LIBRARY
IMPROVEMENT
THROUGH
DATA ANALYTICS

D1564371

ALA Neal-Schuman purchases fund advocacy,
awareness, and accreditation programs
for library professionals worldwide.

LIBRARY
IMPROVEMENT
THROUGH
DATA ANALYTICS

LESLEY S. J. FARMER
ALAN M. SAFER

Neal-Schuman

An imprint of the American Library Association

CHICAGO   2016

ISBN: 978-0-8389-1425-0 (paper)

Library of Congress Cataloging-in-Publication Data
Names: Farmer, Lesley S. J., author. | Safer, Alan M., author.
Title: Library improvement through data analytics / Lesley S.J. Farmer, Alan M. Safer.
Description: Chicago : ALA Neal-Schuman, an imprint of the American Library Association, 2016. | Includes bibliographical references and index.
Identifiers: LCCN 2015046382 | ISBN 9780838914250 (print : alk. paper)
Subjects: LCSH: Libraries—Evaluation—Statistical methods. | Library administration—Decision making—Statistical methods. | Six sigma (Quality control standard) | Library statistics—Case studies.
Classification: LCC Z678.85 .F37 2016 | DDC 025.007/23—dc23 LC record available at https://lccn.loc.gov/2015046382

Cover design by Alejandra Diaz. Imagery © Shutterstock, Inc.

Text composition by Dianne M. Rooney in the Chaparral, Gotham, and Bell Gothic typefaces.

♾ This paper meets the requirements of ANSI/NISO Z39.48-1992 (Permanence of Paper).

Printed in the United States of America

20 19 18 17 16   5 4 3 2 1

Contents

Tables and Figures

TABLES

FIGURES

PART I

Overview

1

Introduction

I can't find the articles I need!

What does it take to get a new book on the shelf before it becomes old?

No one uses our self-checkout system.

Should we subscribe to ebooks?

Why are students just using Google and Wikipedia?

How do we show the value of the library to our organization?

These questions are just a sampling of concerns that library communities ask. Mindful of budget constraints, libraries have to optimize their operations in order to provide the most cost-effective services. At the same time, librarians need to respond to community needs to optimize clientele use and satisfaction. Increasingly, libraries are having to demonstrate their value, and data-driven decision-making is expected of library management. These sometimes conflicting demands may be daunting. Data analytics provides a tested way to assure continuous library improvement. This chapter explains the basis for data analytics, highlighting quantitative aspects, and states how it can benefit library management. A library case study concretizes the use of data analytics to show library value (Soria, Fransen, & Nackerud, 2014).

LIBRARY IMPROVEMENT

In the midst of putting out library brush fires, the idea of library improvement seems like a distant ideal. Just maintaining the status quo can be a library manager's mindset, especially during economic downturns. Perhaps the issue of library improvement comes to the fore during trustee meetings or mandated five-year plans. On the other hand, most librarians do seek to provide the best cost-effective programs of resources and services to meet the interests and needs of their communities. And there's always room for improvement. In fact, hard times require librarians to take a close look at their operations to make them more cost-effective and value-added in the eyes of their communities.

Continuous library improvement calls for an ongoing cycle of planning, action, monitoring, evaluation, and reflection. Although annual reports and major campaigns can serve as touchstones, attention to ways to improve libraries should occur routinely. At first glance, improvement might be envisioned as a bigger collection, more events with greater participation, increased staffing, and increased hours of operation. However, bigger is not always better. Moreover, library improvement can occur without adding resources, and even if resources are reduced. The ultimate criterion is increased value in terms of the best return on investment.

Management circles tend to focus on a subset of continuous improvement: continuous quality improvement (CQI). This ongoing process evaluates how organizations work, and has the intent of reducing waste, increasing efficiency, and increasing satisfaction. The underlying philosophy asserts that problems emerge from ineffective leadership, work design, or communication rather than from worker intent. The goal of CQI is stable and predictable process results, with reduced process variations. It should be noted, however, that achieving sustained quality improvement requires long-term commitment and effort from the entire organization.

DATA-DRIVEN DECISION-MAKING

In a climate of heightened attention to accountability, institutions and organizations are undergoing increasing scrutiny. Recent economic realities have also driven decision-makers to closely examine their operations' cost-effectiveness. Even without external drivers, libraries want to make good decisions. To that end, decision-makers need to gather and analyze meaningful data, and act upon it. What is the return on investment? The phrase "show me the data" rings loudly.

Such emphasis on data means that processes should have characteristics that are measurable so they can be analyzed, improved, and controlled. Some library functions lend themselves easily to such metrics, for example, information services and circulation. It is usually a straightforward process to count frequencies, reference-fill rate, and time-per-unit. However, softer services such as reader's advisory and instruction are harder to measure beyond the surface level (i.e., whether a person checked out a recommended book, or whether a student located an article). Even story hour attendance tells just part of the data story.

Although a list of assets (both human and material) and activities provides useful information about input, it does not suffice. Administrators and other stakeholders need to know how those assets and activities impact their clientele and community at large. Not only should data be collected about the use of those assets and generated products output, but data needs to be collected about the consequences of such use, such as increased literacy and income (outcome). For instance, libraries traditionally cite collection size and circulation figures, but they also need to ascertain if collection use translates into gains in reading ability, more job marketability, or other measurable outcomes. The result is system-based data-driven management.

One of the issues of this system-based data-driven approach is its open-endedness. Unlike a closed system where all parts are internally controlled, libraries operate in an open system where clientele come and go. Librarians cannot control those clients, either in terms of using the library or in leveraging their library experiences to improve themselves or contribute to society. Even something as elemental as checking out a book does not guarantee that the person will read the book, let alone apply the content read to his life. On the other hand, most people act because they think they will benefit from their action, even if it is to enter the library to get out of the rain.

Fortunately, librarians can take this independent action into consideration when making data-driven decisions. Librarians can do an environmental scan of their community to ascertain its status and needs. Census figures can give information about neighborhood demographics, health, income, educational attainment, industry sectors, and so on. School data also gives socioeconomic and demographic data. Local entities such as the Chamber of Commerce and realty companies also keep useful data. These data signal strengths that the library can leverage; for instance, if athletics brings money and attention to the community, then the collection should reflect that emphasis, and library programs can incorporate sports topics and guest speakers. If unemployment is high, then career services might be ramped up. The library can then collect baseline data about the library and community, and then improve its collection and service, re-measuring those data points to see if the library has contributed at least indirectly to the community's welfare. Thus, both internal and external data provide direction for library efforts, and can show the library's value to its clientele and community.

A CASE FOR QUANTITATIVE APPROACHES

Data take many forms: numbers, text, pictures, stories, products. Even politicians know that facts and figures can impress the head, and that a compelling anecdote can move the heart. At the end of the day, though, librarians need to make an evidence-based case for their library programs, and quantitative data need to form the basis for their stances.

Even at the descriptive level (such as identifying mean, mode, range, variance), data can inform decision makers. For instance, data might reveal that the public library is frequented most heavily in the afternoon, with half of the users being high schoolers. The library might well be poised to add reference staff and add YA novels to the collection. But first, librarians should find out the reason for such attendance by surveying users and interviewing local school librarians and other youth-serving agencies. Perhaps the school library closes immediately after the last class—can the public librarian advocate for longer school library hours, or cosponsor library programs? Perhaps few after-school activities are available in the community; could the public library partner with community agencies to do outreach activities or start interest and service clubs? Survey data might reveal that student library users tend to use the library as a place to hang out, which might lead to after-school library clubs; on the other hand, if the main purpose is to study, then the library might establish tutoring services. In any case, quantitative data provide the basis for further investigation and thoughtful analysis.

Descriptive statistics basically summarizes and describes data. Although descriptive data comprise much of library data analysis, the real power of data emerges when using more sophisticated inferential statistics to test hypotheses about populations and predict population characteristics. Inferential statistics can also explore relationships between factors at a more nuanced level. For instance, what is the relationship between library use and corporate profit? A positive significant correlation between these two variables can lead to assumptions about the library's value (although a causal relationship is much harder to prove). Factor analysis can identify the most important library services relative to student achievement. Regression analysis might inform librarians about optimum length of times for training.

Quantitative data not only provides more in-depth internal analysis, but it also enables libraries to benchmark with comparative institutions locally and nationally. With the same kind of data measured in the same way, libraries can find out if their budgets or staffing are equitable, for instance. Furthermore, factors such as socioeconomics can be held constant, so that libraries in disadvantaged neighborhoods can still show that they make a difference in their communities relative to their high-income suburban counterparts.

However, few librarians have a solid statistical background. Statistics is not routinely taught in high schools, and is not a hot course in college. Few library preparation programs delve deeply into quantitative data and its analysis. Even master's programs tend to discuss statistics at the descriptive level (such as mean, mode, variance), and are most likely to work with surveys and numerical data generated automatically by library integrated management systems (such as holdings and circulation figures) and subscription database aggregators (such as access and download numbers for journal titles). Fortunately, librarians do not have to be statistical wizards, and when conducting data analysis should seriously consider getting help from local statistics experts in higher education (including graduate students). On the other hand, librarians should be competent consumers of research and statistics in order to make sense of data, and optimize its usefulness.

BENEFITS OF QUANTITATIVE DATA ANALYSIS

The benefits of quantitative data analysis for library improvement almost always result in a good return on investment. The systematic approach helps to prioritize and target efforts, thus optimizing time management. Data analysis can result in the most bang for their buck because performance and productivity improve, and quality is controlled, so not only are expenses reduced, but satisfaction by staff and users increases.

This sample case study demonstrates the power of quantitative data analysis. A university library wanted to deal with staff budget reductions and resource allocations as it impacted student service desk hours. Specifically, library administration wanted to reduce scheduling time, reduce schedule change, reduce errors, and improve student morale. Student staff scheduling, which was done by a non-student permanent staff member, was very labor-intensive. Some of the issues included need for flexible work schedules because of academic demands, and specific skills needed at specific times. It was determined that the students should do their own scheduling, but there were concerns about lowered productivity. To analyze the data, library administrators used a cause-and-effect matrix that weighed the effect of combined inputs and outputs based on relative importance. They then created a failure model and effect analysis to calculate a risk priority number (RPN) for each input/output process: SEV (severity of effect to customer), OCC (failure frequency), DET (how well failure is detected): SEV × OCC × DET = RPN. The highest RPNs emerged for emailing schedules for review, second highest RPNs were associated with schedule jockeying, and other risk priorities included knowledge of work requirements, human error, competing interest, emailing for student availability, and rehiring marginal students. Based on the analysis, library administrators created three levels of expertise, made a scheduling process template with a set skill level (including a new student supervisory level) and student number for each hour, determined the number of hours students could sign up for, and let high-performing level 2 and 3s sign up first. As a result of the changed scheduling process time involved in doing scheduling decreased, processes were streamlined, and human errors disappeared. The process also led to clearer expectations as well as closer supervision and assessment (Jankowski, 2013).

WHAT THIS BOOK PROVIDES

This book is intended to serve as a practical introduction to data analytics as a means for library improvement.

- Part I concludes with a basic model for library improvement, Six Sigma, and its variations are explained in chapter two.
- Part II includes five chapters, each of which details of the Six Sigma steps for improving library operations and customer satisfaction.
- Part III deals with data. Chapter eight explains how to clean data, chapter nine discusses how to match data with appropriate data analysis techniques, and chapter ten serves as a statistics primer.
- Part IV consists of 14 case studies that exemplify different library functions and associated data analysis.

With this book in hand, librarians can venture into the world of data, and leverage its use for informed, effective library improvement that positively impacts its stakeholders.

REFERENCES

Jankowski, J. (2013). Successful implementation of Six Sigma to schedule student staffing for circulation service. *Journal of Access Services, 10*(4), 197–216.

Soria, K. Fransen, J., & Nackerud, S. (2014). Stacks, serials, search engines, and students' success: first-year undergraduate students' library use, academic achievement, and retention. *Journal of Academic Librarianship, 40*(1), 84–91.

2

Planning with Six Sigma

Data analysis might be an interesting intellectual endeavor in itself, but its power lies in its leverage to take effective action. As such, data analysis comprises one aspect of library planning and management. Not that data analysis is a stand-alone step. Deciding which data to collect, how to collect data, and what to decide as a result of the data analysis all impact the success of data analysis.

Several planning models incorporate data analysis. However, for targeted library improvement, one of the most effective data-driven models is Six Sigma. This model focuses on processes, which provide a rigorous foundation for library program direction and implementation. Although Six Sigma is known more in business circles, it works well in the library environment. However, it is not a management panacea; this chapter lists critical conditions for its appropriateness and success, and ways to adapt some of its practices that fit local circumstances.

HISTORICAL DATA-DRIVEN MANAGEMENT MODELS

As libraries have grown in size and complexity, the need for systematic management approaches has also grown. In general, library administration has drawn from other disciplines such as business and public policy. Data-driven administration probably has its roots in scientific management, which focused on empirical evidence to increase worker efficiency. This systemization of monitoring led to ideas of quality control and operations research.

However, data-based management also extends to the idea of knowledge management: systematically using information to make appropriate and timely adjustments so that organizations can respond to internal and external changes and act strategically. The goal continues to be optimal organizational practice and improvement.

In the 1980s, total quality management (TQM) became popular in the business sector. The underlying idea was to institute an organization-wide climate of continuous improvement to deliver high-quality products and services cost-effectively. Top management has ultimate responsibility for quality improvement, which includes not only systematically monitoring processes but also leading and supporting all the employees. Quality itself is ultimately defined in terms of the target clientele: their needs and wants.

One aspect of TQM is statistical process control: measuring processes to optimize quality and minimize variation (quality control) (Wheeler & Chambers, 2010). To that end, the variables of each process need to be identified and measured, such as the supplies (quality, cost) and their interface or combination (such as attaching a spine label on the book); labor (performance quality and quantity, salary) and their interaction (e.g., one step to another, collaboration, etc.); and the work environment (e.g., furniture, traffic flow, lighting and air quality, etc.). Each variable is analyzed and controlled so that the entire process can be optimized. Each process can be considered as a micro-system, contributing to the overall system of the organization.

Several current management models focus on organizational improvement through a cycle of planning, implementation, study, and action that focuses on data analysis.

After World War II, the US Navy applied statistical process control to its own operations, which formed the basis of the US Department of Commerce's Baldrige Performance Excellence Program. The Baldrige Excellent Framework helps organizations assess their performance management system by measuring and analyzing the effectiveness of their leadership, workforce, operations, strategy, and customs to attain optimum results.

Largely supplanting TQM, ISO 9000 consists of a collection of standards. ISO has an international trade focus, and examines the links between suppliers and insurers. ISO 9000 is based on eight management principles that insure that organizations meet legal product requirements.

Kaizen, which means "continuous improvement," started after World War II in Japanese businesses. Its philosophy is that improving standardized activities should involve all employees in identifying and eliminating waste in all organizational functions. Kaizen promotes employee-initiated small scientific experiments to make and monitor change rather than top-down large projects. Kaizen also incorporates quality circles in which employee teams take responsibility for suggesting and making changes. The steps involved in Kaizen include: standardizing operations, measuring, comparing, innovating, and upgrading the standardization.

The Lean approach focuses on cutting out waste, and using only value-added process steps. The ultimate measure is customer satisfaction: Is the person willing to pay for the product or service? The main steps in the Lean approach include: analyzing opportunity, planning improvement, focusing on improvement, and improving and delivering performance.

SIX SIGMA

Six Sigma is the most well known of these data-driven models for organizational continuous improvement. The business sector in particular uses Six Sigma as a management tool to optimize cost-effective practices, control quality, and increase customer satisfaction by using data to identify problems and their causes, and then identify workable solutions. As such, Six Sigma has several key attributes: customer focus, data driven, rigorous process improvement methods and tools, professional development, full time resources, strategy execution, and quantifiable results (Galganski & Thompson, 2008).

Six Sigma was conceived by Bill Smith, a Motorola Corporation reliability engineer. He realized that complex organizations include many processes, each of which might have a sizable failure rate. Because processes can impact each other throughout the system, the rates could multiply and the resultant failure rate could end up being very significant. Smith asserted that to maintain quality control, any one process should have an error or failure rate that is six standard deviations from the norm: less than 3.4 defects in a million units. When such high standards are met, productivity and profits increase, and clientele are likely to value the organization more. Because standard deviation is symbolized mathematically as a small sigma, σ, the term Six Sigma was coined to capture the essence of improvement goals in this approach.

The management principle behind Six Sigma is one of data-based enterprise-wide involvement and resource allocation. As such, Six Sigma includes two main models: DMAIC (Define, Measure, Analyze, Improve, Control), which is used for improving existing processes; and DMADV (Define, Measure, Analyze, Design, Verify), which is used for developing new processes.

DMAIC

The following steps detail DMAIC (Brassard et al., 2002).

1. *Define the project.* The organization's stakeholders identify a project that is likely to result in significant improvement relative to the resources required to get those results. The group clarifies the project's purpose, scope, and value. Then the group documents background information about the process under scrutiny and the impacted clientele. With these data, the group can identify which resources are required and available. Taking into account the clientele's expectations, the group then determines the key characteristics by which to measure success. Next, the group develops a written organizational agreement and a communication plan, including an intended timeline. With the high-level process outlined, the implementers are chosen: leaders, managers, and impacted staff.

2. *Measure the current situation and performance.* At this point, the project team investigated the identified problem in detail: what the problem is or where it is happening. This process requires collecting baseline data, so the team has to determine which data are essential to collect in order to identify the defects/problems and their possible causes; what are the key performance indicators? The team also has to decide which tools to use to collect those data. With this information, the team can see how the current process operates, and decide on targeted improvement performance level, which becomes a focused problem statement.

3. *Analyze the problem's root causes, and collect evidence to support that stance.* Using the collected data, the team applies statistical methods to find cause-effect relationships between processes and results. Statistics enables the team to test multiple causes of the program, such the specific patterns found relative to materials, human actions, and working environment. The team also determines the process's capacity to accomplish its task (i.e., are there enough staff to conduct a library orientation for every freshman class). Once the team comes to agreement on the cause of the problem, they can address that cause by hypothesizing feasible solutions.

4. *Improve performance.* At this point, the team plans and tests interventions that can address the problem's root causes. Before-and-after data for each intervention are collected and analyze the compare performance. In some cases, an intervention makes no difference, which means another solution must be found. In terms of management skills, preparing staff for change must also be planned at this step.

5. *Control the process by standardizing practice.* The team seeks to maintain consistent high-quality performance. To this end, the improved practice is documented, and affected staff are trained to implement that process competently and consistently. Performance needs to be closely monitored at this time to identify and rectify deviations. The team also creates a process for updating procedures and anticipating future improvements. They also review efforts, and share lessons learned.

DMADV

DMADV follows similar steps. However, the chosen project focuses on a new initiative that needs to be developed, rather than improving an existing one. At the analysis step, the organization looks as the process options. At the design step, instead of an improvement step, the determined process is designed in detail. Then, instead of a control step, a verify step checks the design process and its ability to meet the identified needs.

Arizona State University's interlibrary loan process exemplifies the DMIAC model and its benefits (Voyles, Dols, & Knight, 2009).

Goal: To embark on a strategic project to assess the service quality and cost of filling interlibrary loan journal article borrowing requests.

Define: The Document Delivery Team's goal in this phase was to gain a clear understanding of the interlibrary loan (ILL) process, in order to improve its turnaround rate and cost-effectiveness for periodical articles. Their premise was that no additional staff or money would be required to meet their goal.

Measure: The Document Delivery Team created a flowchart of the ILL process; gathered ILL activity sheets; and set up a performance matrix to identify inputs and outputs, key success factors, quality standards, and cost for each step. The team interviewed the associated staff about the ILL process.

Analyze: The team's goal in this phase was to make sense of all the data gathered in the measure phase. The team created a fishbone diagram of contributing factors. They also produced a histogram that visualized the percentage of requests not filled in three days, which uncovered the program with weekend request fills. A subsequent Pareto chart verified that weekend lending was the root cause of lag time. They found that student workers executed the weekend ILL process because no permanent staff were present then. Drilling down, data revealed that student workers had difficulty choosing the right ISSN. Furthermore, difficult requests were set aside, a situation mainly experienced by the student workers.

Improve: The team recommended and tested the following solutions: having other evening and weekend permanent staff do ILL during their downtime, adding permanent staff hours on evening and weekends, training all relevant staff on ILL procedures, replacing student workers with full-time temporary staff, adjusting scheduling, and encouraging other libraries to increase their own evening and weekend ILL staff and use the consortia's union catalog more often.

Control: A follow-up XmR control chart highlighted data point patterns, which revealed decreased turnaround time after staff were trained and permanent staff were added to the weekend schedule. The control chart continued to be used to monitor ILL performance to insure sustained quality.

Results: The Six Sigma DMAIC approach resulted in an improved interlibrary loan borrowing journal article process. The modified process showed a cost saving of $2.09 per request, even with a 16% increase in borrowing requests. Furthermore, all interlibrary loan article deliveries were changed to be done electronically to clienteles' desktops, and turnaround time for article delivery was reduced to 70% of filled article requests being delivered in three days or less.

WHEN TO USE SIX SIGMA

No one program improvement process fits every situation, and Six Sigma is no different. When fully implemented, Six Sigma requires leader commitment to the project and to the dependence on data to make decisions. When Six Sigma teams have the capacity and support for innovative thinking, and the entire enterprise is involved, then results are likely to be more fruitful. People who use Six Sigma techniques should know about statistical process control techniques, data analysis methods, and project management. In its full manifestation, Six Sigma organizations incorporate specific, aligned training and certification for different project roles, and typically involve a corporate cultural change. However, Six Sigma's basic steps and many of its data collection and analysis tools may be applied to a variety of settings without subscribing to the entire package or using advanced statistics. Indeed, sometimes the library's capacity may be too limited to use certain data analysis methods. On the other hand, larger library systems can enlist the help of statisticians, such as university faculty, to help with some of the more sophisticated data analysis methods.

In the final analysis, cost-effective library improvement requires a systematic approach. Data are needed to describe and document current conditions, and facilitate analysis and decision making. Data provided the foundation for identifying reasonable interventions and measuring their impact. Elements of Six Sigma provide a workable framework for organizing efforts to problem solve efficiently and optimize improvement.

REFERENCES

Brassard, M., Finn, L., Ginn, D., & Ritter, D. (2002). *The Six Sigma memory jogger II.* Salem, NH: GOAL/QPC.

Galganski, C., & Thompson, J. (2008). Six Sigma: An overview and hospital library experience. *Journal of Hospital Librarianship, 8*(2), 133–144.

Voyles, J. F., Dols, L., & Knight, E. (2009). Interlibrary loan meets Six Sigma: The University of Arizona Library's success applying process improvement. *Journal of Interlibrary Loan, Document Delivery and Electronic Reserves, 19*(1), 75–94.

Wheeler, D., & Chambers, D. (2010). *Understanding statistical process control* (3rd ed.). Knoxville, TN: SPC Press.

PART II

Six Sigma Steps

3

Defining the Project

S ubstantial pre-planning and negotiation occur even before deciding on the specific goal and defining the project.

WHAT SHOULD IMPROVE?

What is worth improving? That's a major question that library staff should ask when they monitor and review how they use their resources. Certainly it is a question to ask when writing up annual reports, addressing accreditation issues, or developing a strategic plan. Indeed, library improvement may be considered a mindset, especially for library managers.

On the other hand, there is a risk of "getting lost in the weeds" of problems, or spending all available time putting out brush fires. Determining what to pay attention to, and what to act on, is a critical skill. Making such a decision should not be a solitary endeavor, but rather the result of collaborative consideration of major stakeholders.

When considering a concerted improvement effort, library decision-makers should review their mission statement, determine how well the library's program, resources, or services align with that mission statement, and then ascertain the quality of those resources and services. Most libraries are accountable to an umbrella organization, such as an educational institution or a corporation, as well as to some board such as trustees, and their mission and programs should also align to that superior entity.

Librarians should examine their internal practices as well as their external environment, including competing organizations. This environmental scan should consider the library's strengths and weaknesses, external threats, and opportunities. Librarians can also benchmark their programs with other comparable libraries. Nevertheless, the bottom line is community satisfaction and improvement.

CHOOSING RELEVANT DATA

Data about processes, products, and perceptions are crucial throughout the process: from the needs assessment at the beginning to the assessment of the implemented improvement intervention. Data may be derived from content analysis, observation, work analysis, surveys, tests, benchmark data, interviews, and focus groups. Fortunately, there is an abundance of existing data that librarians can access.

Some internal data points include:

Acquisitions: the bases and processes for selecting materials and vendors, licensing options, ordering tasks, materials processing tasks, cataloging tasks

Collection holdings: volume, date, cost and budget, physical condition by material type and subject, number of missing and lost items, physical arrangement, preservation and conservation functions, deselection functions

Circulation: by material type, user demographics, checkout length of time, overdues, holds and reserves, in-house use, shelving processes, turnaround time

Computer hardware and software: quantity, currency, physical condition, specifications and standards, upgrading and updating, access by staff and users, Internet connectivity, maintenance functions, technical support, and cost and budget

Internet: connectivity; speed; broadband width; Wi-Fi, LAN, and WAN; cloud service; technical support; maintenance; cost

Other technologies: (e.g., copy machines, faxes, scanners, camcorders, mobile devices, and peripherals): quantity, currency, specifications and standards, physical condition, access by staff and users, maintenance functions, technical support, cost and budget

Library website: purpose, functionality, accessibility, content, layout, interface, updating function

Library publications: purpose (e.g., instruction, signage, information, publicity), types (e.g., bookmarks, flyers, handbooks, posters, newsletters, press releases, reference guide sheets), formats (e.g., print, banners, video, audio, website, and multimedia presentation), content, production tasks, dissemination function, cost and budget

Reference: location(s), interface (e.g., face-to-face, email, instant messaging, synchronous online), hours of operation, staffing patterns (e.g., quantity, qualifications, tiered service), user demographics, types of questions, resources used (and available), length of each reference interaction, and reference fill rate

Instruction: quantity, time frame, one-shot versus series, location(s), user demographics, staffing patterns, mode of instruction (e.g., face-to-face, online), groupings (individual, small groups, large groups, class), scheduling (e.g., on demand, set period), repeat business, academic or functional unit (e.g., chemistry, accounting, new employee training), instructional content and purpose, staffing patterns (e.g., instructor title, subject specialist), learning aids (e.g., adaption or creation, format, access, storage, usage, review/revising), planning function, assessment function

Internal communication: purpose, content, audience, quantity, frequency, creation function, format, and dissemination function

Staffing: quantity, qualifications, recruitment and hiring function, length of service, retention and promotion processes and patterns, salaries, supervision function, organizational structure, governance

Staff training and development: basis and purpose, format, frequency, time frame, trainer patterns, standardized versus customized, in-house versus outsourced, just-in-time versus scheduled, documentation, accountability, assessment, and cost and budget

Facilities: location(s), square footage, physical condition, maintenance function, utilities usage, security, exterior (e.g., landscaping, parking), furniture, traffic flow, service centers, and usage patterns (by space, time, user demographics)

Some external data points include:

Community demographics: census information (household size, ages, income, ethnicities, educational attainment, health), block/ZIP code population density, land use, building use, transient rate, and crime rate

Local services and agencies: transportation, telecommunications, social services, health services, parks and recreation, educational services, police services, and emergency services

Commercial situation: industry sectors, economic indicators (profit, employment rate, stability), entertainment, cultural offerings

Governmental-political situation: governance structure and practice, laws and regulations, political parties, and civic engagement quality

In addition, libraries need to gather data about their parent/supervising entity.

EDUCATIONAL INSTITUTIONS

Staff: demographics, experience, qualifications, years of experience, site retention rate, in-service development, library use

Students: demographics, languages, academic record, retention and graduate rate, post-graduation plans

Curriculum: mission, scope, subjects, content, texts, instructional strategies, learning activities, assignments, library role, co-curriculum

Time factors: calendar, operating hours, scheduling

Support services: health, technology, safety, maintenance, fiscal

Administration and governance: committees, boards and trustees, decision-making practices, policies, procedures

BUSINESS

Management: mission, vision, policies, procedures, planning, evaluation

Personnel: demographics, experience, qualifications, years of experience, site retention/promotion rate, in-service development, library use

Functions/units: human resources, management, accounting, marketing, public relations, sales, customer service, supply chain management, technology, facilities and maintenance

Clientele: demographics, needs and interests, degree of satisfaction

Regardless of the source or the data collection method, the data need to be valid, that is, they must measure what is intended, for example by using a gate counter to determine the number of library users physically in the facility. On the other hand, borrowing statistics are not a valid measure of resource use because in-house use may account for the majority of use in some settings. Similarly, the length of time that a person sits in front of a computer might not be a valid indicator of how much the computer is used. Data must also be reliable; that is, if the same measure is used another time, will the answer be the same? If two different librarians analyze the same document, will they code it the same way? A simple example of non-reliability is a malfunctioning timer.

MAKING DECISIONS

In examining the library's potential, librarians should identify those factors that are essential for success. What are the non-negotiables, particularly as perceived by the community? What operating hours are essential: specific days of the week, after school, during the day for retirees and daycare? Depending on the demographics of the community, the library may need to provide collections and services to meet its needs, such as children's materials and story hours for family-centric libraries; technical manuals and industry trade publications for corporations; support materials for new school curricula; scholarly journals; and instruction on databases for academic libraries. Businesses may need quick turnaround time for ILL and competitive intelligence research, while school libraries need to teach students how to evaluate websites.

These critical success factors provide a guide to collect data and assess the library's current ability to provide a high-quality, cost-effective program. Identify what most frustrates library users and staff, because these critical areas signal high-priority needs and goals, and form the basis of the library's improvement plan. Data provide the concrete evidence of practice, and can help operationalize those improvement goals. What would success look like? For instance, drawing upon the above examples, businesses may need a turnaround time of 72 hours for document delivery. Perhaps every freshmen English class course might require students to write a short informational report using peer-reviewed articles, which means that librarians must instruct all those students. Identifying one significant area for improvement tends to maximize improvement and input, as opposed to trying to manage a handful of little projects. Ideally, the plan should focus on a far-ranging issue that impacts several staff and functions of the library, such as materials processing, instruction, or knowledge management.

The plan itself requires a careful collection of stakeholders: experts, suppliers, influencers, and managers. This planning team should include library staff, at least one organizational administrator or manager, a representative from each affected unit, a couple of key influential library users, probably a fiscal agent, a data expert, and capable clerical and technical support. The team should reflect a variety of expertise and a commitment to work together towards attaining the goal. The team needs to negotiate roles and responsibilities, establish communication protocols, determine decision-making processes, identify time and effort commitments, and develop their monitoring and assessment process. The team also needs to motivate the enterprise to actively engage in the improvement efforts. Foremost in culling buy-in is the message that all employees contribute to the enterprise as a whole, and that the project is trying to provide the optimum conditions so that staff can accomplish their work effectively and be proud of their work.

At this point, the major points of the improvement plan can be outlined. The plan should define the project goal and specific objectives, its scope, the deliverables, the efforts and risks involved. The planning team needs to identify the material, fiscal, and human resources available—and any other additional resources that are needed—to attain the goal. Does the library have the capacity to meet the goal? What contingency plans may be made? For example, the library might not have enough qualified staff to provide a 1-hour face-to-face workshop for every freshman English class, particularly at times that meet the scheduling needs of English teachers; however, available librarians might be able to conduct and record webinars about locating database articles, or create a screencast for faculty and students to access. Flowcharts can help visualize the steps, and help identify possible gaps and their causes. A project grid (e.g., table 3.1) such as a PERT or Gantt chart can clarify actions, people or units responsible, time frame, resources, data, and assessment.

TABLE 3.1

Project Chart

	Week 1	Week 2	Week 3	Week 4	Week 5
Task A					
Task B					
Task C					
Task D					

4

Measure the Current Situation

A t this step, the project team develops metrics and specifies the project goals, based on in-depth knowledge about the current situation.

MATCHING THE OBJECTIVE AND THE DATA

In order to answer the project questions "What are the root causes of the problem?" and "How will we solve the problem?" the project team needs to collect valid and reliable data that they can use to analyze the problem and identify effective interventions that solve the problem.

Table 4.1 suggests feasible types of data for different functions and issues. Representative measurements of performance follow (Summer, 2007):

Clientele: number of clientele, repeat business, new users, time to resolve customer service customer complaints

Finance: revenues, expenses, cost per unit, profitability, return on investment

Process: improvement in task turnaround time, improvement in quantity, completion rate, improvement in quality, cost savings

Staffing: employee retention and promotion, cross-training success, morale

TABLE 4.1

Processes and Matching Data

Function	Factors	Data sources
Collection development		
Requests	Workflow, lead time, error	Requests, emails, purchase orders
Vendors: publisher, jobber, bookstore	Cost-benefit analysis, time analysis, error	Selection plans, purchase orders and supporting documents including fill rates, license agreements, budget
Fit of collection	User satisfaction, usage, ILL	Selection plans, circulation figures, on shelf count, requests, ILL figures, reserves, student work, faculty research, user/ non-user survey, budget
Acquisitions	Decision, workflow, lead time, cost-benefit analysis, failure analysis	Purchase orders and supporting documents, license agreements, work analysis, observation, rubrics, interviews, focus groups, budget
Processing	Workflow, lead time	Process analysis, product analysis, observation, rubrics, interviews, focus groups
Cataloging	Workflow, lead time, staffing, in-house versus outsourcing, error, customer satisfaction	Process analysis, product analysis, observation, rubrics, interviews, focus groups, user survey, reference desk observation and survey, web usability study, reference desk counts
Access	Process analysis, process capacity, customer satisfaction	Website hits, web usability analysis, think-aloud process, screencast think-aloud process, website heat maps, process analysis, observation, user surveys, interviews, focus groups, reference desk counts
Circulation	Workflow, customer satisfaction	Process analysis, product analysis, circulation figures, snags, observation, rubrics, interviews, focus groups, user survey
Overdues	Workflow, failure analysis	Process analysis, product analysis, circulation figures, on shelf analysis, budget
Shelving	Workflow, work cell, lead time	Process analysis, on shelf analysis, observation, rubrics, interviews, focus groups
Preservation	Decision, workflow, lead time	Process analysis, product analysis, observation, rubrics, interviews, focus groups, budget
Digitization	Decision, workflow, lead time	Process analysis, product analysis, observation, rubrics, interviews, focus groups, budget
Format choice (print versus ebooks)	Decision, cost-benefit analysis, workflow, lead time, customer satisfaction	Circulation figures, library catalog hits and download figures, user surveys, requests, selection plans, budget, processing analysis

Function	Factors	Data sources
Collection development (cont.)		
Own versus access	Decision, cost-benefit analysis, workflow, lead time	Circulation figures, library catalog hits and download figures, observation, user surveys, selection plans, budget, processing analysis
Interlibrary loan	Workflow, failure analysis, cost-benefit analysis, time analysis, error, customer satisfaction	Process analysis, product analysis, ILL system records, observation, rubrics, interviews, focus groups, user surveys, budget
Weeding	Workflow, lead time, error	Deselection policy, process analysis, product analysis, observation, rubrics, interviews, focus groups, user surveys, budget, cataloging processing analysis
Website		
Interface: ADA, layout, functions, customization	Customer satisfaction, decision, cost-benefit analysis	Website hits, web usability analysis, think-aloud process, screencast think-aloud process, website heat maps, process analysis, observation, user surveys, interviews, focus groups
Content: type of content, posting	Customer satisfaction, workflow, error, staffing	Website hits, think-aloud process, screencast think-aloud process, website heat maps, process analysis, observation, user surveys, interviews, focus groups analysis
Mobile format: choice of software, functionality	Customer satisfaction, decision, cost-benefit analysis	Website hits, web usability analysis, think-aloud process, screencast think-aloud process, website heat maps, process analysis, observation, user surveys, interviews, focus groups
Technology resources		
Computers: #, length of time, scheduling, wait time, installations, Standardized versus customized	cost-benefit analysis, queuing, customer satisfaction	Observation, process analysis, schedule records, technical standards and specifications, user surveys, interviews, focus groups, purchase orders, budget
Other equipment use by patrons: copy machine, self-checkout, scanners, etc.	cost-benefit analysis, customer satisfaction	Observation, process analysis, schedule records, reserves, technical standards and specifications, user surveys, interviews, focus groups, purchase orders, budget
Maintenance	Lead time, in-house versus outsource, workflow	Observations, process analysis, product analysis, user surveys, interviews, focus groups, repair records, invoices, budget

(cont.)

TABLE 4.1
Processes and Matching Data (cont.)

Function	Factors	Data sources
Reference		
Bibliographies: creation, posting/ dissemination	cost-benefit analysis, customer satisfaction, decision	Observation, process analysis, product analysis, website hits, document requests, reference desk use, user surveys, interviews, focus groups, supplies orders, printing counts, student works' and faculty research bibliography analysis, budget
Format choice	cost-benefit analysis, customer satisfaction, decision, staffing, training	Reference desk counts, website hits, IM counts, reference interaction transcripts, user surveys, observation, interviews, focus groups, budget
Reference fill: resources used/available, interaction	Customer satisfaction, workflow, failure analysis	Reference desk counts, website hits, database usage figures, IM counts, reference fill rate, reference interaction transcripts, user surveys, RUSA rubrics, observation, interviews, focus groups, budget
Staffing	Cost-benefit analysis, customer satisfaction, decision, location analysis, tiered reference, scheduling/queuing, qualifications needed	Reference desk counts, website hits, IM counts, reference locations, reference interaction transcripts, queuing analysis, user surveys, RUSA rubrics, observation, interviews, focus groups, budget
Reference collection: choice of items, extent	Cost-benefit analysis, workflow, failure analysis	Reference fill rate, reference interaction transcripts, database usage figures, collection figures, reference resources reshelving, user surveys, RUSA rubrics, observation, interviews, focus groups, budget
Hours of operation	Cost-benefit analysis, customer satisfaction, decision	Reference desk counts, observation, user surveys, interviews, focus groups
Instruction		
Developing presentations/ handouts: standard versus customized	Workflow, cost-benefit analysis	Benchmarking, process capability analysis, process analysis, product analysis, content analysis, dissemination figures, printing figures, observation, user surveys, interviews, focus groups, budget
Format: online tutorials, F2F, web conferencing	Cost-benefit analysis, customer satisfaction, decision	Benchmarking, process analysis, learner assessment, observation, instruction requests, user surveys, interviews, focus groups, budget
Location: library, class, virtual	Cost-benefit analysis, customer satisfaction, decision	Benchmarking, room use figures, process capability analysis, learner assessment, observation, instruction requests, user surveys, interviews, focus groups, budget
Scheduling	Workflow, failure analysis, customer satisfaction, lead time	Instruction/scheduling request and fill rate, observation, user surveys, interviews, focus groups

Function	Factors	Data sources
Instruction (cont.)		
Collaboration with faculty	Customer satisfaction, cost-benefit analysis	Benchmarking, instruction/scheduling request, lesson plans, learning aids, observation, user surveys, interviews, focus groups
Repository of presentations and lessons	Cost-benefit analysis, customer satisfaction, decision, workflow	Contributions to repository, peer reviews, repository hits, course syllabi, process analysis, product analysis, user surveys, interviews, focus groups
Impact on student achievement	Cost-benefit analysis, customer satisfaction	Student work analysis, grades, retention and graduation rates, observation, user surveys, interviews, focus groups
Communication		
Internal	Failure analysis, satisfaction	Mode count, frequency count, content analysis, process analysis, observation, user surveys, interviews, focus groups
Between staff and clientele: mode (F2F, reps, librarian liaisons, print, online)	Cost-benefit analysis, workflow, customer satisfaction, decision	Mode count, frequency count, content analysis, process analysis, product analysis, dissemination figures, printing figures, observation, user surveys, interviews, focus groups, budget
Staffing		
Hiring	Workflow, lead time	Process analysis, applicant documentation and demographics, retention and promotion rates, observation, user surveys, interviews, focus groups
Staffing/scheduling	Process capacity, failure analysis	Process capacity analysis, process analysis, queuing analysis, user surveys, staff retention and promotion rates, observation, interviews, focus groups, budget
Training: format, frequency, standardized versus customized, in-house versus outsourced, JIT versus scheduled	Cost-benefit analysis, customer satisfaction, decision	Process analysis, instruction/scheduling request, attendance records, lesson plans, learning aids, room use figures, learner assessment, observation, instruction requests, user surveys, interviews, focus groups, budget
Evaluation	Workflow, tolerance/failure analysis	Process analysis, content analysis, retention and promotion rates, observation, user surveys, interviews, focus groups
Accounting	Workflow, failure analysis	Fraction non-conforming
Facilities		
Traffic	Flow analysis	Observation, GPS analysis, user surveys, interviews, focus groups

(cont.)

TABLE 4.1

Processes and Matching Data (cont.)

Function	Factors	Data sources
Facilities (cont.)		
Security	Failure analysis	Observation, security records, collection inventory (e.g., lost and missing items), user surveys, interviews, focus groups
Maintenance	Failure analysis, cost-benefit analysis, customer satisfaction	Observations, process analysis, product analysis, user surveys, interviews, focus groups, repair records, invoices, utility bills, budget
Disaster management	Decision, workflow, lead time	Training records, process analysis, supplies inventory, drill records, loss and recovery inventory, observation, user surveys, interviews, focus groups, budget
Landscape	Decision, cost-benefit analysis	Observation, GPS analysis, physical condition, process analysis, user surveys, interviews, focus groups, budget

As the project team identify appropriate data, they should consider the following factors:

- Whose data are being collected: library workers, administrators, other employees, library users, library vendors and suppliers, families, the community at large, the entire population or a sample (representative or targeted)?
- Who collects the data: project team, library workers, administrators, other employees, trained volunteers, statisticians, outside consultants?
- When does data collection occur: before, during, or after planning; before, during, or after a process; before, during, and after an intervention; before, during, or after a library visit; at the start and end of a reporting period; at a specific time of day or week?
- Where does data collection occur: in libraries, in classrooms, in offices, in meetings, in public spaces, at home, online?
- How is data collected: by survey, observation, test, rubric, interview, focus group, work analysis, usage analysis, systems analysis?
- Who analyzes data results: project team, personnel in affected units, other librarians, other administrators, statisticians, outside consultants?

INSTRUMENTATION

Data is only as good as the instrument used to collect it. Good reviews of the literature help librarians determine the contributing factors that impact the issue under study. Assessment instruments that have been validated can be adapted for local issues, reducing or eliminating instrument development time. Research articles offer tested methodologies, and even ineffective techniques can help avoid the same failures. Reading the data analysis and discussion helps librarians how to leverage findings to make recommendations.

Locating research about data instruments and their use follows the usual steps:

1. *Choose relevant keywords*
   - Who is the target audience: learners, administrators, reading specialists, service groups?
   - What is the setting: library, educational setting, social service agency, corporation?
   - What is the goal or objective?
   - What is the possible root cause of the issue: staffing, material resources, training, lack of support, inefficient processing, funding?

2. *Choose appropriate resources*
   - Scholarly: Research articles, dissertations, conference proceedings
   - Comprehensive: books, bibliographies, encyclopedias
   - Timely: newspaper, television, blogs
   - Human: professional associations, interviews

3. *Access relevant information within resources*
   - Research purpose and questions
   - Context: setting, timing, community, need or problem
   - Methodology: procedure for selecting population and collecting data
   - Data analysis
   - Conclusions and recommendations

4. *Evaluate resources*
   - Validity: author/agency credibility and agenda, rigor of methodology, quality and quantity of data and instrumentation, conclusions, implications, timeliness
   - Relevance: alignment with the improvement project
   - What worked and what didn't—and why; what advice is given

- Feasibility of duplicating the process: cost, timeframe, staffing needs, resource needs, use of facilities
- Impact on the library and its users

Usually, the project team should use an existing validated instrument, even if it needs to be slightly modified to fit local conditions, rather than develop one from scratch. Existing instruments save time and effort, and if used by comparable libraries, can facilitate benchmarking.

Much of library practice involves processes, and frequently these processes cross or impact several functions. For instance, the process of acquiring materials involves subject librarians who read reviews of new publications and get requests from their clientele, the business unit who deals with purchase orders, and the cataloger who weighs in on MARC record profiles if the item includes that product. Even within one function unit, a process may require several steps, as when processing a new book (covering, reinforcing, labeling, placing a security strip). Each time an item or document is handled, value is added—and mistakes can happen. Therefore, when conducting a process analysis, each step needs to be specified and inspected to see if it is done correctly or not. A time stamp and the name of each person involved can also be noted.

Likewise, a product analysis can serve as a summative evaluation to ascertain any faults. For instance, in original cataloging, each record's field is a source of possible error. Similarly, an evaluator can examine all the books processed at the end of the day using a simple checklist to mark mistakes or missing elements as shown in table 4.2.

TABLE 4.2

Book Processing Elements

Elements	Errors	Notes: total 30 books
Book jacket	Wrong size /// Missing tape	Cover is too large (ran out of the correct size??)
Inside page reinforcement	Missing // Sloppy	
Spine label	Upside down Wrong call number ////	Call numbers are cut off—at wrong digit too
Bar code	Wrong placement Wrong number	
Stamp	Missing title page Missing page 15 ///// Illegible //////	Is stamper going too fast? Do we need a new ink pad?
Security strip	Missing Visible //	

5

Analyze Existing Processes

The next step involves analyzing the collected data to identify patterns and reveal the root causes of problems. The analysis leads to making recommendations about ways to solve the problem and improve practice. Several methods may be used to clarify the data.

ANALYSIS APPROACHES

The easiest scenario is one in which one area for improvement stands out, such as high printer ink expenses. A "five whys" method can uncover the root cause, as illustrated here in a simple case.

1. Why is there a high printer ink expense?
   Because the printer runs out of ink so fast.
2. Why does the printer run out of ink so fast?
   Because so much printing is done.
3. Why is so much printing done?
   Because students print out long encyclopedia articles.

4. Why do students print out long encyclopedia articles?
   Because they don't know how to select only a section to print out.
5. Why don't students know how to select just a section to print out?
   Because no one showed them how to use that feature.

The solution is to inform students via training classes and posting directions on the computer. The library could limit the number of pages printed or even disable printing, stating that students must download and save documents onto a thumb drive or school directory, but these alternative solutions do not address the problem. Of course, a different reason for each "why" statement would result in a different cause and solution (e.g., multiple copies being printed because no copy machine exists; the printer model is not ink-efficient, and another model might be more cost-effective, etc.).

Most libraries start by applying descriptive statistics to organized data in an effort to reveal patterns or trends. Typical generated statistics include:

Range: from low to high; for example, the number of circulation of DVD titles from zero (*My Life as a Sock*) to 87 (a Disney movie)

Mean or average: such as the average number of library visitors per week

Median: the mid number of all the observations (e.g., the number of reference questions per day, collected for the month), which is sometimes a more accurate reflection when the distribution of frequencies is not even

Mode: the more frequently occurring number, such as the size of audience for story hour over 2 months.

Table 5.1 shows the raw data and the generated descriptive statistics for the story hour example. Each statistic tells a story.

TABLE 5.1

Story Hour Attendance

	Week 1	Week 2	Week 3	Week 4	Week 5	Week 6	Week 7	Week 8	Week 9	Week 10
Attendance	5	8	9	2	22	5	10	7	5	7

- Range: 20 (22–2)
- Mean: 8
- Median: 7
- Mode: 5

What is the story behind the data? Week 4 had a snow day, and week 5 included a make-up day with a special magician (the figures for these days are considered outliers). There's a core group of five attendees/families. If the number of weeks were increased (i.e., there were more observations), more descriptive statistics could be generated, such as quartile information (the bottom, mid, upper, and top quarters of the data) and standard deviation (showing variability, that is, the degree of data heterogeneity or homogeneity). As the example shows, the data by themselves do not explain patterns; additional data are needed, such as the weather conditions in this example. Data might show patterns of library use by time period (e.g., less on the weekends, more in the afternoon), and then the project team will need to gather more data—perhaps by interviewing staff and library users—to find out why such patterns occur and to determine if there is need for improvement.

One major aspect of data power is missing with descriptive statistics: relationships. When two sets of data, such as two questions from the same survey, are compared, then a clearer picture emerges. For example, comparing library use by time of day and general age (e.g., child, teen, adult, senior citizen) using correlation statistics may find that teens use the library more in the afternoon, and seniors visit more in the morning, so that staffing scheduling can be adjusted to meet those target population's needs more effectively. Such inferential statistics can show the degree and significance of relationships between two or more populations. As the sampling size of that population increases, the distribution of that sample approximates a normal distribution, allowing a variety of powerful parametric statistics to be applied. Even though causality is very hard to prove (e.g., if you visit the library more frequently you will become a better reader), finding a positive significant relationship (e.g., families who visit the library weekly are more likely to read more) is informative, and, in this example, might be a good selling point for the public library to co-sponsor a workshop at school about family reading. Representative statistical methods are detailed in the next chapter.

When a process consists of several steps or factors, the team can design an experiment to test the different factors (independent variables) to see which one makes a difference in the resulting output (the dependent variable). The experiment can use existing data for historical information, or the team can perform a series of tests to gather and analyze new data. In either case, the team first identifies all the possible variables that are likely to impact the output. They also have to choose the level of data; in some cases, a first data sweep leads to the realization for the need of more detailed data collection. A fishbone diagram (see figure 5.1) can help visualize possible sources of error.

A simple example is cataloging a book. Variables might include:

1. Whether the book is physically present, or if the cataloger is copy-cataloging from another source of information
2. The book's subject matter
3. Language of the book

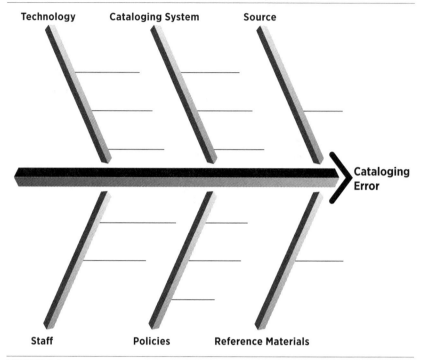

FIGURE 5.1
Fishbone Diagram

4. CIP: whether it is present or not, if the information is correct, if the information is relevant
5. Cataloging software program: its functionality, characteristics of the input mode, technical robustness
6. Cataloger: expertise, training, physical condition
7. Reference materials: availability of AACR2 or RDA, subject headings authority document, classification system authority document
8. Turnaround time

The team should note which variables can be controlled (e.g., availability of reference materials) and which cannot (e.g., CIP availability). Data collected about the catalog records might reveal that the chief errors are incorrect subject headings. Each variable can be tested to see if it is related to the subject heading mistake. Here are a couple of possible scenarios.

Time: Does the length of time to catalog the book result in incorrect subject headings? If yes, then perhaps when the cataloger rushes, she doesn't analyze the book carefully enough. Either the cataloger should be more thorough, and perhaps the cataloger needs training to ascertain the correct subject heading more quickly.

Subject matter: Does the subject matter of the material result in incorrect subject headings? If yes, then the team can drill down to see which subjects are more likely to lead to errors. If, for example, science topics are miscataloged more than others, then the recommended action might be to ask a science expert to help identify the subject. This added step will take more time, but if it leads to a higher retrieval rate, it might be worth the extra time involved because cataloging is intended to be a onetime function per item or unit.

CIP: Does the presence of CIP information result in incorrect subject headings, all other variables being held constant? If yes, then further experimentation is needed. If the CIP is missing and the subject headings are more likely to be wrong, then the cataloger needs to catalog from scratch, or she might consult another source of information, which the team must find out by asking the cataloger. Often times, smaller publishers do not submit their books to the Library of Congress for CIP inclusion; these publishers typically have niche titles that might be harder to analyze, resulting in inaccurate subject headings—which would depend on the expertise of the cataloger on site, or the cataloger who creates a MARC record that the site cataloger uses. Because several sources of copy cataloging exist, an appropriate intervention might be for the cataloger to compare the quality of several cataloging sources and choose the most reliable one to copy—or depend on her own knowledge. The cataloger may state that original cataloging takes more time, so that turnaround time will be impacted. The project team and cataloger have to decide whether accuracy is more important than time saved; they can calculate the cost per unit for cataloging, measure it against time needed to find a miscataloged book, and determine the relative return on investment. It is likely that a longer cataloging time is more cost-effective because it is a onetime cost, as compared to each time that someone has to locate a miscataloged book. If, on the other hand, when CIP is available and the subject headings are more likely to be wrong, then further examination is needed. A probable cause is the misalignment of the CIP subject heading authority (the Library of Congress) and the use of a different subject heading authority by the library (e.g., Sears). An interview with the cataloger may reveal that she did not get adequate training to differentiate between the Library of Congress and Sears system, or to use Sears subject headings. Perhaps the library does not have the Sears reference available, or owns an outdated edition. Each of these causes then enables the team to make a logical recommendation about ways to improve the process.

Several variables might be identified as significant. The project team can decide which has the highest priority as measured by cost (usually due to length of time, translated into salary cost), frequency of error, or impact of error (e.g., retrieval failure by a significant percentage of users). It is usually easiest to implement one intervention, measure its effectiveness, and control its quality. Then the next intervention can be implemented until the total error rate is within acceptable range. This example also points out the need for expertise in analyzing the data. Only a highly knowledgeable cataloger or subject librarian is likely to identify miscataloged books; lacking that expertise, the evaluator might benchmark the cataloging with another reputable catalog that uses the same cataloging system (e.g., classification system and subject headings system).

A factorial design experiment is useful for identifying main effects (i.e., response change by a change in the factor's level) when several factors, or variables, exist. The resultant digital data set can include demographic information (e.g., gender, age range, student/faculty status, major), as well as specific information about frequency and timing of library visits, services used, resources used, training or assistance, and degree of satisfaction for each element. A factorial design can test all possible combinations of the factors (e.g., service used and major) and their respective levels (e.g., high versus low usage, high versus low satisfaction). When the level of one factor is significantly different at various levels of the other factors, an interaction is revealed. This interaction can mask a main effect, so is important to explore; it can be a confounding variable. For instance, students may visit the library more frequently as they progress through college (a main effect), but in combination with the training, they may cancel each other out. By looking at the main effect of library visits at different levels of training, it might reveal that students who get more library training visit less often because they know how to find library materials online, so they can access needed resources remotely without the need to visit the library. Without combining the two factors, the project team might make the wrong recommendation for library improvement. As can be imagined, when more than two factors interact, ferreting out the underlying issues can be very challenging.

Another way to analyze the data is to benchmark it, as has already been mentioned. The basic idea is to compare data with a similar setting to identify possible areas of improvement. Similarities typically include characteristics such as similar socioeconomic status, service area population figures, facility size and age, number of volumes, operating hours, number of staff, and budget. The closer the similarity, the more effective the benchmarking. For instance, if a comparable library has twice the circulation as the project's library, then the factors that contribute to that difference need to be explored. If all the aforementioned characteristics are essentially the same, then differing factors need to be teased out, such as analysis of the collection (e.g., by subject, format, intended audience, currency); facility specifics (e.g., displays, location of circulation desk); story hours, class visits, events, book clubs, meetings (e.g., frequency, attendance, collection tie-in, off-site events where participants can check out materials); staff (e.g., reader's advisory practices, booktalks, outreach activity, bibliographies); policies (e.g., number of items that can be checked out at one time, fines and their impact on borrowing privileges, age-specific borrowing limits, lending time frame, borrowing policies on periodicals and reference materials). Such brainstorming of possible factors will usually involve visiting the other library or interviewing its staff to gather relevant data to help draw inferences that can be acted upon.

HYPOTHESIZING THE SOLUTION

By analyzing the data in detail, the project team can narrow down the possible causes of the problem, or identify the area for improvement, to the point that they are confident about the root causes and can address those causes with reasonable assurance. Here are ten generic causes and feasible solutions.

- Lack of knowledge → train
- Lack of awareness → publicize and inform
- Poor visibility → change location, move furniture, create displays
- Lack of space → reconfigure space, deselect unnecessary items, incorporate remote storage
- Slow turnaround time → streamline process
- Poor fill-rate by vendor → compare with other vendors' fill rate for comparable titles
- Long queues at the reference desk → add reference staff, post signs for frequently asked directional questions, develop a ticket procedure or sign-up sheet, post alternative ways to get reference help
- Unsatisfactory scheduling → change process, change or train scheduler
- Slow computers → do thorough maintenance (e.g., disc scan, clean), upgrade or replace computers
- Lockout of subscription databases (too many simultaneous users) → change license agreement

As with researching data instruments, librarians can also conduct a literature review of solutions to their problems. By knowing the root cause, they can refine their searches to locate relevant articles, and even contact the featured library to gain insider tips.

In some cases, the solution may require added material, human, or fiscal resources. If the team can show cost savings, time savings (which ultimately results in cost savings), or cost-effective return on investment (such as greater user satisfaction and perceived greater value) that is evidenced in the data analysis, then those added resources and support may be easier to procure. This situation is another reason to include a key decision-maker on the project team.

In other cases, the library may simply not have the capacity to meet its users' demands. For instance, it might not have the space, budget, and trained personnel to provide 3D printer service. However, librarians should try to find out which local institution might have such a service, and negotiate with them to enable library users to access that service. If the demand grows for 3D printer service, librarians should document it, and consider it along with other priorities in their long-term plan so that they can plan for staff and space changes strategically.

REFERENCE

Summer, D. (2007). *Six Sigma: Basic tools and techniques.* Upper Saddle River, NJ: Prentice-Hall.

6

Improve or Introduce the Process

Now that the project team has identified the probable root causes, and hypothesized ways to correct them, the team can reexamine the targeted processes or practices and figure out how to introduce the specific interventions or changes. The goal is to have an improved process that is stable and predictable, and that meets users' needs. The baseline data helps the team measure the impact of the changes on the critical output; usually, the same type of statistical analysis can be applied.

GENERIC PROCESS IMPROVEMENT STEPS

At this point the team has brainstormed solutions, evaluated them, and selected those they consider to be optimal. Their next step is to develop a "to be" value stream map that shows what the process will look like after the changes are made. The value may be considered in terms of cost savings, time savings, improved quality, increased productivity, improved performance, user satisfaction, or other values agreed upon by the organization and community. The team has to make sure that sufficient resources, expertise, and support are available to make the changes.

The team then plans and tests interventions that can address the problem's root causes. Each process is named, its starting and end point are noted, including target output quantity and quality. Each aspect of the process needs to be documented; a flowchart visualizes the steps and helps to capture decision points and possible alternative actions. As the team analyzes and modifies the process, they need to consider several aspects:

Time: start-up or set-up time, work time, wait time, and break-down time

Interaction with other processes: straight-line with no interaction, with the product handed off to the next group after it is completely finished by the first group (e.g., processing a book), or parallel processes where several items can be processed at the same time independently by different groups (e.g., creating content for a webpage while the technical aspects of the webpage are addressed) to come together later

Degree of customization: simplifying the process, standardizing the process (i.e., one-size-fits-all), developing alternative process paths depending on the nature of the item or user (e.g., different interlibrary loan process depending on the type of resource being requested)

Typically, the change is pilot-tested on a small scale: one person, one part of the process, a short time period, one set of products. The team needs to determine the scope of the test; it should also be mentioned that the scale needs to be large enough to be measureable and analyzed. Close monitoring is necessary, and it can be useful for the staff handling the process to think-aloud what they are doing. An observer taking field notes can be debriefed after the pilot study. The project team also has to take into account that lead time may be needed, and the pilot process may actually take more time than previously because new skills and habits need to be learned. Before-and-after data for each change are collected and analyzed to compare output. In some cases, an intervention makes no difference, which means another solution must be found or the scale needs to be greater to achieve measurable improvement.

A run chart is one way to track data over time, and shows whether a solution has significant lasting impact on the process. A key variable is plotted on the y-axis, such as number of book snags or ILL turnaround time, and unit of time is plotted on the x-axis. A run chart can also determine acceptable tolerance rates, such as time to complete a process or an acceptable number of errors, as shown in figure 6.1. The changed process started on day 5.

Once the process has been successfully pilot-tested, to the point that the output is acceptable and has some pattern of consistency, and is supported by convincing data and analysis, the project team can execute a full-scale implementation plan. That final plan takes into account which lessons have

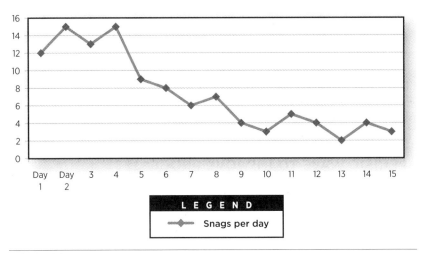

FIGURE 6.1
Run Chart

been learned and what made the solution effective. Procedures must be clear and thorough to enable all workers to succeed in doing the task. Policies that might be affected by the change also need to be reviewed and possibly revised.

In terms of management skills, preparing staff and clientele for change must also be planned at this step. In facilitating change, several conditions need to be considered: readiness for change, knowledge of the current situation, vision and perception of the change, resources and support capacity to support change, leadership and commitment to change, cognitive and affective factors impacting the change process, reinforcement and incentives for change, and factors to ensure sustainability and integration. Management needs to sell the change to all affected staff as well as key internal and external influencers such as department chairs, board members, and key clientele (Pande, Neuman, & Cavanagh, 2014). Some of the techniques for helping people buy into the change include:

- starting with willing and influential volunteers
- creating short-term wins to provide early success that can motivate further change and greater acceptance
- conducting a force-field analysis that shows barriers to change, and design means to overcome those barriers
- storyboarding the change to show its positive impact
- inspiring a sense of purpose and enthusiasm, especially among staff, that emphasizes their empowerment to make a positive difference and contribute to organizational improvement

As with other kinds of communication, communication about change needs to be tailored to each audience to point out the specific benefits to each sector. For instance, establishing virtual reference service means that users can get help from their desktops, which is more convenient for them. For the librarian, virtual reference can mean less waiting time at the reference desk. Fortunately, as change becomes the new normal, it sets up the conditions for further change and improvement.

SPECIFIC WAYS TO IMPROVE PROCESSES

Where does waste occur: in time or resources? Trimming techniques identify possible ways to cut down on waste. In closely examining a process, the project team should identify what value each step has—including the resources used to carry out the step. Are there any extraneous elements, or ones that do not add value to the final product? For instance, can the librarian work on any other projects while at the reference desk, such as updating bibliographies, so that time is managed more effectively? Should reference desk hours be cut when little business is conducted—or should the reference librarian be called if there is a need?

Another way to improve practice is to consider changing the scope of a process or of a person's responsibilities. For instance, libraries often orient freshmen students, but they often forget about transfer students; expanding orientation to this population would be a valuable service. In the special library sector, the same issue emerges, with an added twist; librarians might consider reorienting employees who have been recently promoted or have moved to a different unit; they might not be aware of the domain-specific resources and services that would apply to their new jobs. Scope expansion also applies to added library staff responsibilities, such as adding a similar subject domain to their portfolio of liaison work, or shelvers might also serve as back-up staff at the circulation desk. In all of these cases, the added scope is closely related to the existing one so that it leverages current expertise and requires little added training. Another direction for scope expansion is in terms of resources, such as adding ebooks to the collection, providing 3D printers, or building a professional library for K–12 teachers. Expanding the range of clientele is another form of scope expansion, such as letting parents check out materials from the library (and perhaps setting up a parent corner with parenting materials). Scope expansion comes at a price. Staff may feel that they are being asked to do more with less, so the data need to demonstrate a strong case for such expansion. Data need to show minimal extra work results in significant gains. An example would be a decrease in reference questions because more students can successfully locate materials by themselves, because transfer students attended library orientations. The project team also has to make sure that the library has the capacity to successfully expand the scope of resources and services. For instance, does the library have experts who can explain how to use a 3D printer, and can they troubleshoot and service the equipment? Does the library have the funding to keep supplying the raw material used to make the 3D objects? Any time that scope expansion is being considered, the consequences need to be fully explored first.

Feature transfer involves moving desirable features from one system to another, or moving several features from multiple systems to one system. For example, the discovery function of databases and link resolvers are being increasingly transferred to library catalogs. Typically, when considering transferring features, the project team starts with a base product or process that they are trying to improve, such as virtual reference service. One of the challenges might be the time that it takes a user to find a relevant resource online. An alternative system for virtual reference service is email, which is asynchronous, and is easier for librarians to control than synchronous reference help. The project team might recommend that the virtual reference librarian ask the user for his or her email address so that if it looks as if the search will take some time, the user doesn't have to wait online but can still get the information in a timely fashion.

Failure modes and effects analysis (FMEA) is a method to anticipate possible process or product failures, and figure out ways to prevent or counteract them (Summer, 2007). Those involved in the process, other experts, and possibly key users work together to list each step in the targeted process, and then:

1. Brainstorm potential failure modes (e.g., crashes, illegibility, jams, errors).
2. Identify the potential impact on the key output variables or internal requirements (e.g., delays, defective product), and rate the degree of severity of its effect on clientele.
3. Identify the causes of the failure/effect, and rate its probability of occurrence.
4. Identify the existing controls that either prevent the failure to occur or detect failure if it occurs, and rate how easy it is to detect.
5. Apply the same 1–10 rating scale to all rating decisions, and multiply the three ratings to derive the risk of each failure mode to obtain its risk priority number.
6. Continue the same process for each step—and for each possible failure mode within the same step.

This method helps the project team to prioritize processes to focus on, and to identify specific steps to address.

REFERENCES

Pande, P., Neuman, R., & Cavanagh, R. (2014). *The Six Sigma way: How to maximize the impact of your change and improvement efforts* (2nd ed.). New York, NY: McGraw-Hill.

Summer, D. (2007). *Six Sigma: Basic tools and techniques.* Upper Saddle River, NJ: Prentice-Hall.

7

Control the Process

The team seeks to maintain consistent high-quality performance. To this end, the improved practice is documented, and affected staff are trained to implement that process competently and consistently. Performance needs to be closely monitored at this time to identify and rectify deviations. The team also creates a process for updating procedures and anticipating future improvements. They also review efforts, and share lessons learned.

GENERIC CONTROL PROCESS STEPS

Changes have been made and improvement is apparent, but the work is not over. The project team has to develop the mechanisms and documentation for supporting the change and insuring that its full-scale implementation is sustainable (Pande, Neuman, & Cavanagh, 2014). Documentation needs to include:

- a transition plan for improving the process, for which the process supervisor is responsible
- a system for monitoring implementation solutions

- before-and-after data on the process metrics
- training documents that address scheduling, content, supporting reference materials, assessment
- a feedback mechanism, incorporating both internal and external communication
- product documentation
- lessons learned and recommendations for further action and opportunities.

As noted before, all affected personnel need to be trained. Typically, the supervisor of the improved process does the training for a couple of reasons: he has pilot-tested the intervention and so knows the issues involved in the change, and has the responsibility of making sure that performance and output are high-quality and efficient. It should be noted that training skills are different than both technical skills and management skills. Human resource trainers can work with the supervisor to ensure an effective training process that is both informative and enjoyable. As with the rest of the improvement project, data needs to be collected about the training process: needs assessment, identification of available material and human resources, learning activity, and participant outcome and satisfaction. Of course, the most authentic assessment is performance after the training. As in the pilot-test period, supervisors have to give workers some lead time to become comfortable and competent; the process might take longer than before, but the output should be equal or better than previously. Supervisors should anticipate possible points of error, spot possible confusion, and provide short-term targeted support. Supervisors should also determine action alarms or trigger points in order to identify short-term emergency fixes and make recommendations for further improvements. These problems, and solutions, should be thoroughly documented, and incorporated into the final project's documentation.

The supervisor should also communicate with other groups about training and management experiences and supporting data. Not only should the changed process be monitored closely, and its data analyzed, but other possibly affected processes need to be monitored as well. By informing each other, supervisors and other decision-makers can optimize and accelerate improvement throughout the enterprise. Complex systems such as the library are comprised of many interdependent functions. For instance, if a tech desk is established near the reference desk to take over handling computer questions, do reference traffic and the kinds of reference questions change? If the ILL process shortens turnaround time, does the number of ILL requests increase, possibly impacting the circulation desk workload? The data collected and analyzed from these audits inform the enterprise and suggest the next areas for improvement. There are many ways to review the system as a whole:

walk-throughs, observing library users' behavior and soliciting their feedback, and conducting focus groups with key stakeholders.

Training, user experiences, and cross-function monitoring relative to change provide the bases for locking in performance gains. The first few weeks and months require thorough monitoring and analysis. What are acceptable levels of performance and product? The project team may have over- or under-estimated the difficulty of improved processes or the ease with which change is accepted. As a result, adjustments in expectations may need to be made, or the process under scrutiny might need to be refined to ensure consistent controlled output.

Not only should task data be collected but the team should also talk to staff and users about how they are adjusting psychologically. In some cases, incomplete or unclear communication might lead to confusion or concern, in which case the project team needs to review their messaging content and delivery, and test it out with a few staff and users to measure affect.

As part of the control process, preventative and predictive maintenance need to be addressed. For instance, with increased library use comes increased wear and tear. Bathrooms might need to be cleaned more often, and supplies ordered more often. More signs might need to be posted to help orient new users. Schedules will need to take into account changing fluctuations in library use, such as increasingly popular story hours. Computers might need more stringent configuration settings and weekly disc scanning. If more people bring in their own devices, the library may need to broaden the bandwidth or tighten authentication and online security measures. As much as possible, the project team and the rest of the staff should brainstorm these maintenance issues ahead of time, and take preemptive action.

In the process of monitoring the system, unintended consequences may emerge, for example parking problems due to increased library use. In this situation, the project team will probably have to solve this issue quickly before a backlash occurs. On the other hand, an unintended consequence may be good, such as when the library's improved service may lead to more funding or authorization for additional staff. In any case, the project team—as well as the rest of the staff—should be on the lookout for surprises, which they can then measure and address.

PROJECT EVALUATION

The project team, staff, library users, and other stakeholders all want to know and to be able to assess how effective improvement projects have been in meeting their goals. Data-based success can be measured along a couple of dimensions (Rossi, 2007):

The process: how well the project itself was planned and implemented

The project's outcome: what impact improvement has on its participants, both the library staff and other stakeholders

In any case, many questions arise when assessing an improvement project's effectiveness:

CLIENTELE

- How many were impacted?
- What was the quality of the impact?
- Who were not impacted or did not participate—and why?
- What did participants think of, and feel about, the project?
- How has the clientele changed as a result of the improvement?

OUTPUT

- Was the outcome high-quality and valued?
- Was the process well designed?
- Was the training appropriate?
- Was its implementation effective?
- Was the working environment appropriate?
- Were resources used effectively?
- Was it cost-effective?

LIBRARY

- How effectively were library resources used?
- How did the project support or advance the library's mission?
- How did the project change library services or resources?
- What did library staff learn from the project's planning and implementation?
- How did the project impact the library's relationship with stakeholders?
- To what degree was the project worth the library's effort?

PLANNING

- Did all planners participate and make decisions appropriately?
- Was planning done productively?
- Did the planning address identified needs?
- Did planners have positive interpersonal relationships?
- Were resources used wisely?
- How would planners build on the process in the future—or make changes?

When the project team finalizes the project, they validate performance and determine fiscal impact. The results should be cost-effective. The report should also note evidence of buy-in and stakeholder acceptance. Indeed, part of closing the project loop involves revisiting the library's core processes and clientele, identifying clientele needs, and measuring current performance. The project's report should be widely communicated and celebrated. The project team should remember to share the project and its successes all along the way, not only with the staff but also the stakeholders and the community at large. Improvement helps everyone.

REFERENCES

Pande, P., Neuman, R., & Cavanagh, R. (2014). *The Six Sigma way: How to maximize the impact of your change and improvement efforts* (2nd ed.). New York, NY: McGraw-Hill.

Rossi, P. (2004). *Evaluation: A systematic approach.* Thousand Oaks, CA: Sage.

PART III

A Statistics Primer

8

Cleaning Data

There is a common saying in analytics about data: garbage in, garbage out, which is also referred to as "GIGO." In essence, if the data are not cleaned, then no matter how fancy or complex the statistical analysis, the results will be garbage. There are many components to cleaning the data, but some of the cleaning involves making sure the analysis does not involve bad data—among many other possible checks. These include: (a) typos, (b) extreme observations, (c) inappropriate assumptions for analysis (and thus making appropriate transformations on recoding of the data), and (d) deleting observations or imputing (i.e., estimating) missing observations. Consequently, it is extremely important to spend an appropriate amount of time on the data before doing the full analysis and then interpreting of results.

The data being used to exemplify the cleaning process come from the American Association of School Librarians' School Libraries Count! survey conducted in 4,278 schools in the United States in 2012. The survey included 60 questions involving various aspects of each of the school's libraries. The annual survey took place in 2007 and aimed to measure the health of the school libraries in the United States. The 2012 survey included additional questions that focused on filtering online content for students.

SETTING UP THE DATA

A common starting place for analyzing data is to input the raw data into a spreadsheet with the columns as the variables (e.g., number of library books, budget, number of librarians, etc.). The rows of the spreadsheet are individual observations (e.g., individual libraries), or if the data describe one library, the observations might involve gathering data on individual days. The first row would have the column headers (variable names). For example, if dealing with a survey, the first row may include something like Question 1 (Q1) name of library, Q2 location, Q3 number of librarians, etc. The spreadsheet shown in table 8.1 begins to show the values for individual observations (in this example, libraries).

Most spreadsheet programs have a data view and a variable view, so that the meaning of each piece of data can be stated clearly, and its data type (e.g., numeric, string) clearly identified. For some variables, such as Q4 in table 8.1, the responses can be recoded as numbers (e.g., 1 = elementary school, 2 = middle school, 3 = high school) to facilitate data entry and analysis. These groupings or recodings then need to be documented in the variable view of the spreadsheet. Alternatively, people may input string (character) data (such as dates), which codes the data.

Once the data are structured, some of the variables may be removed if they are not necessary for the analysis. This constitutes the variable reduction step. For example, if the name of the school is not going to be used in the analysis, it should be removed. In the AASL dataset with 44 starting variables, 6 variables were removed to insure confidentiality or because the variable was deemed trivial (e.g., filtering software is required).

Additionally, sometimes it helps to create new variables from original ones to make the resultant variables more usable. For example, using the total number of hours employed and the number of teacher-librarians, a new variable was created reflecting the number of hours per teacher-librarians. In the example data set, six variables were created based on the current variables.

TABLE 8.1

Start of the Spreadsheet Including Data on Individual School Libraries

Q1 library	Q2 location	Q3 number of librarians	Q4 collection level	Q5
Newcomb	Long Beach	3	High School	
Wilson	Palo Alto	7	Middle school	
Thompson	Oakland	4	Elementary	

The next step in data cleaning is to fill in missing values, such as city and ZIP code. In the example data set, missing values were filled by referencing another data set that had both the information provided in other parts of the survey (e.g., school name, state, and website) as well as the missing data. In this case, the missing values for the Title I school variable were filled in using National Title I Association's web-based data set. Similarly, the National Center for Education Statistics (NCES) data set provided missing location information.

INITIAL EXAMINATION OF THE DATA

A first statistical examination of the data may lead to eliminating, modifying, or recoding some of the data in order to provide a more meaningful analysis. A good place to start with data is to do descriptive statistics for the quantitative variables. Common useful descriptive statistics include the minimum, first quartile, median (second quartile), third quartile, maximum, the mean (average), and the standard deviation (which reveals variability). So, the descriptive statistics for overall flexible hours include:

- Minimum = 0
- First quartile = 5.00
- Median (second quartile) = 20.00
- Third quartile = 36.00
- Maximum = 51
- Mean (Average) = 20.53
- Range (maximum—minimum) = 51
- Standard deviation = 15.77
- Sample size = 3984

One useful graphing technique for quantitative data is the box plot (see figures 8.1 and 8.2), which shows quartile and range information.

When the overall data are divided by school level, the box plots in figure 8.2 show a very different picture than revealed by the graph above. The middle and high schools have distributions where a majority of the schools are above the primary school level. For high schools, over 75% of the schools are above the third quartile of primary schools. In middle schools, the first quartile is just below the third quartile of primary schools.

For qualitative (categorical) variables such as state, looking at the frequencies of the individual categories is a good way to analyze the variable. Bar charts (figure 8.3) facilitate comparing subgroups, and pie charts (figure 8.4) show proportions of a whole. A Pareto chart (figure 8.5) graphs the categories from most common to least common, and shows the cumulative percentage on the same graph.

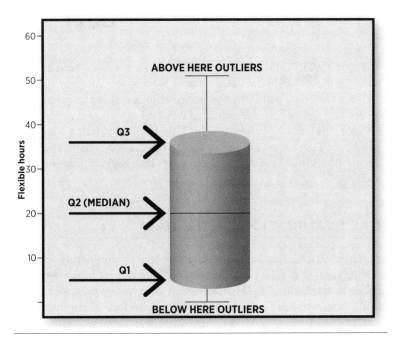

FIGURE 8.1

Box Plot for Overall Number of Flexible Hours

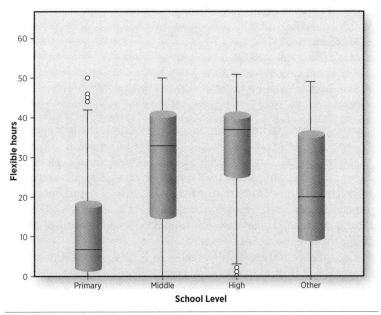

FIGURE 8.2

Box Plot for Number of Flexible Hours by School Level

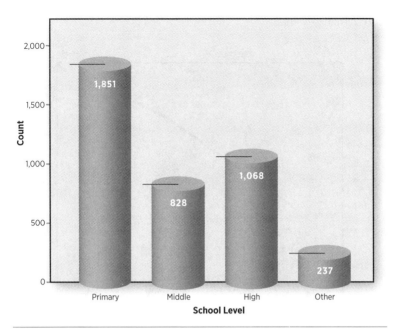

FIGURE 8.3

Sample Bar Graph Showing Number of Survey Respondents
by School Level

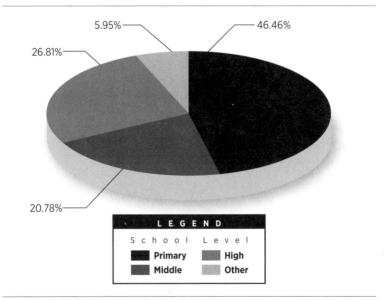

FIGURE 8.4

Sample Pie Chart Showing the Percentage of Survey Respondents
by School Level

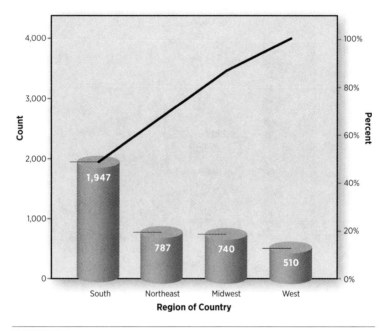

FIGURE 8.5
Pareto Chart of Library Regions

This Pareto chart shows the regions of libraries participating in the survey. From highest participation to lowest participation, they are the South (1,947, 48.8%), Northeast (787, 19.8%), Midwest (740, 18.6%), and the West (510, 12.8%). If library patrons were asked which aspects of the library need improvement, the responses could be put in a Pareto chart similar to this, but with those types of responses from high to low along with the corresponding cumulative chart above the histogram (see figure 8.6).

DEALING WITH OUTLIERS

Looking at the univariate tables and associated graphs gives a better feel for the distribution of the data. Are the data, for example, bell-shaped (normal), uniform, or bifurcated? One way to deal with extreme observations (outliers), as shown in figure 8.2, is to remove a small percentage of them so that these data points will not unduly influence the analysis. For box plots the observations X are considered extreme (outliers) if either are true:

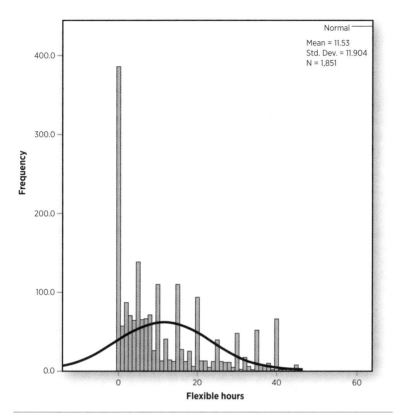

FIGURE 8.6

Histogram of the Distribution of the Number of Flexible Hours
at Primary Schools

$X < Q1 - 1.5*(Q3\text{-}Q1)$ OR $X > Q3 + 1.5 * (Q3\text{-}Q1)$
(again, where Q1 is the first quartile, and Q3 is the third quartile)
when the distribution is not normally distributed.

If a variable is approximately normally distributed, then any point either more
or less than three standard deviations from the mean is an outlier (<0.3% of
the data are this far away from the mean for bell-shaped data). For instance,
the distribution of the variable "flexible hours for primary schools" is not bell-
shaped (i.e., not normally distributed). In fact, the data are considered to be
skewed to the right as there are a few high values, even though most are relatively low (see figure 8.6).

Using the statistics in table 8.2 for the variable, flexible hours, and the
appropriate formula based on the distribution of the variable, outliers can be
easily determined.

TABLE 8.2

Descriptive Statistics for the Distribution of the Number of Flexible Hours at Primary Schools

n	Valid	1,851
	Missing	0
Mean		11.53
Standard deviation		11.904
Minimum		0
Maximum		50
Percentiles	25 Q1	2.00
	50 Q2 (median)	7.00
	75 Q3	18.00

If the variable is approximately normal, then look at values that were less than -24.812 (i.e., mean – 3 * standard deviation, 11.53 – 3 * 11.904 = 24.812) and consider them as outliers. Values above 47.242 (i.e., mean + 3 × standard deviation, 11.53 + 3 * 11.904 = 47.242) would also be considered as outliers. The reason for this designative is that 99.7% of data from a distribution that is approximately normal is within three standard deviations of the mean (i.e., mean – 3 × standard deviation < value of flexible hours < mean + 3 × standard deviation). So, any value outside of these deviations would be considered an outlier because less than 0.3% of a normally distrusted variable would be outside three standard deviations from the mean.

However, the data on figure 8.5 do not fit the bell-shaped normal distribution—which is graphed on top of the histogram as a curve. So, looking at data points either three standard deviations from the mean above or below is not valid. Instead, when data are not normally distributed, a different formula for outliers is needed. In the example noted in table 8.2, the 75th percentile (Q3) is 18.00. The 25th percentile (Q1) is 2.00. So, if any value for flexible hours is less than -22, [i.e., 2.00 – 1.5 * (18.00 – 2.00)], or any value for flexible hours is greater than 42 [i.e., 18 + 1.5 * (18.00 – 2.00)], then this value would be considered an outlier. In this case, there are no possible values below 0 for flexible hours. So, there are no low outliers. However, there are five values above 42. So, there are five high outliers (observations 1,877, 1,598, 1,560, 1,613, and 702).

Once an outlier is identified, then the next step is to determine what to do with those extreme points. If a data point value is, for example, 9,999, it is likely that this value is a code for something missing that was inputted by a person entering the data into the computer program or spreadsheet. If a value for an observation is impossible, say the number of librarians at a particular library equals 100, maybe there was a typo and the number really should be 10 (or even 1). So, it is important to check each entry if the data are entered manually by having a person other than the person who entered the data verify each entry (which might be done by checking the relevant website or data set, or by contacting the respondent). If these efforts are not fruitful, then it becomes necessary to make a decision on whether or not to delete that observation. The advantage of having a big data set is that such observations can be more easily deleted, and there will still be enough data to analyze.

In order to remove any effect that the outliers might have on this particular library analysis, the top 0.5% of the data were removed from 23 variables with the most extreme data. This action removed about 6.87% of the data. It was decided not to remove the bottom 0.5% of the data, which tended to have a low value of zero.

A final way to deal with an unusual observation is to do what is called *imputation*: estimating the true value of that data point based on all the other data points. This action is commonly done in surveys that involve sensitive questions and have high nonresponse, such as income of a person or weight of a person. However, it can also be very useful when the data point does not involve a sensitive subject, but rather when the data points are unknown because of a typo, when there is no way to check the original value, or the data point was mistakenly left blank.

RECODING VARIABLES

Sometimes it is helpful to transform a quantitative variable to a qualitative variable. For example, if a survey asks how many years the person has been a librarian, that data might be more meaningful if the number for years are clustered: for example, 0–10 years, 10–20 years, 20–30 years. For budget numbers, it might be more useful to convert the raw figures into categories of low, medium, and high. In the sample data set, it may be helpful to look at spending per student and analyze the levels by low (less than $5), medium (between $5 and $15), and high (higher than $15).

After looking at the univariate tables and graphs, it can be helpful to look at bivariate tables (contingency tables) for qualitative variables. For example, to see the relationship between budget and the number of librarians, a contingency table of low-medium-high budget versus low-medium-high number of librarians can be generated, and then a statistical test can be performed to determine if a significant relationship exists.

In any case, it is important to check the data set thoroughly before going to any analysis. This includes cleaning the data and graphing the data. If there are problems with the data, there are steps that can be taken to correct issues. There are particular graphs for different types of data, and it is important to use the appropriate ones.

9

Getting Started with Statistics

Once the project team has a clean raw data set, possibly augmented by related data sets, the question arises about which statistical techniques are possible, and what kind of resulting interpretation can be done. This decision is very important yet not widely understood. Say, for example, that a survey has 10 questions, and 1,000 librarians fill out the survey. In addition, assume that two pieces of extra information about the librarians (e.g., length of service, credential status) have been added. Then the dataset would have 12 columns (for the variables) and 1,000 rows (one for each librarian). So, each row would represent a survey filled out by one particular librarian. Among the coding processes is identifying what type of variable each question (variable) in a survey represents: qualitative (categorical) or quantitative (numerical values with meaning). What kind of statistic is appropriate, and what kind of analysis can be applied? Ideally, the research questions drive the kind of data to collect and how to analyze that data.

DESCRIPTIVE STATISTICS

Before doing any analyses, it is important to first find descriptive measures of each quantitative or categorical variable before attempting to reach the research goals. Common descriptive statistics include mean, median, mode, five-number summary, standard variation, variance, range, and 95% confidence interval.

Central Tendency: Mean, Median, Mode

Some of the main values for measuring central tendency of a variable include the mean, median, and mode. The mean is just the statistical term for the arithmetic average. The values over all observations are added up, and that sum is divided by the number of observations. For example, assume that there are five libraries and a certain number of audiobooks per school. Assume the following observations for each of the five libraries: 45, 52, 30, 80, 67. Then the mean is (45 + 52 + 30 + 80 + 67)/5 = 274/5 = 54.8.

The median is the middle number. First, order the numbers from low to high, and then find the middle number, in this case: 30, 45, 52, 67, 80. The median in this example is 52. The example includes five observations, which is an odd number of observations, and the median will always be the middle one for an odd number of observations. For an even number of observations (e.g., six observations), order the numbers and then average the middle two numbers to find the median. The median tends to be a better representation of the measure of central tendency if there are any outliers (i.e., extreme numbers) because the median is not affected by outliers, unlike the mean.

The mode is the number that occurs most often. If there is no number that occurs more than once, then there is no mode. It is possible to have more than one mode. The mode is generally more useful for categorical data. Note that neither the mean nor median can be calculated for categorical data. However, it is possible to determine all three measures of central tendency for quantitative data. In the above example, assume that there are elementary, middle, and high school levels. The five observations are: middle, middle, high, primary, middle. Then the mode is middle school because it occurs more times than high school or middle school.

Measures of Spread or Dispersion

For quantitative variables, descriptive statistics can be determined for measures of spread or dispersion.

The most basic measure of spread is range, which is the difference between the largest (maximum) value for the variable in the data set and the smallest (minimum) value. For the example about audiobooks, the range would be 80 – 30 = 50.

A better way to measure the spread of the data is using what is called the *standard deviation*. The standard deviation is the square root of the average sum of the squared differences from the mean. For the above example of five data points for audios in the library, the mean is 54.8. To determine the standard deviation for the five data points

1. Take the difference from the mean for each data point, then square the difference, and sum them up:

   $[(45 - 54.8)^2 + (52 - 54.8)^2 + (30 - 54.8)^2 +$
   $(80 - 54.8)^2 + (67 - 54.8)^2] = 1502.8$

2. Divide that sum by the sample size, in this case 5:

   $1502.8 \div 5 = 300.6$

3. Take the square root of the result (i.e., quotient) in step 2:

   $\sqrt{300.56} = 17.3$

The standard deviation is 17.3. The variance is just the standard deviation squared, $17.3 \times 17.3 = 300.6$.

This calculation assumes that the five data points are all the points in the population. However, if the data represent a sample, there would be a small correction for calculating the sample standard deviation (and variance). Instead of dividing by the amount in the sample, a person would divide by the sample size minus 1 to account for what is called a loss of *one degree of freedom*.

Five-Number Summary

Percentiles were discussed in a previous chapter: Q1 (25th percentile, 50th percentile [the median], 75th percentile). A common way to describe the data for a quantitative variable is to use the five-number summary, which consists of the minimum, Q1, median, Q3, and maximum.

In the library survey data set in table 9.1, the variable audio books reveals the following descriptive statistics.

The five-number summary states the minimum = 0, Q1 = 12, median = 45, Q3 = 100, maximum =136. Along with the mean being 82.82, it is noted that the mean is somewhat bigger than the median, and there are some rather high values including the maximum of 1,361. The standard deviation of 125.27 is somewhat high compared to the mean of 82.82. Assume that a quiz for a class is normally distributed, with a mean of 70 and a standard deviation of 5. This situation assumes that most (about 95%) of the scores are within 60 and 80 (two standard deviations from the mean). If the standard deviation was smaller, this would indicate that the scores are closer together (less variation).

TABLE 9.1

Five-Number Descriptive Statistics Summary

n (sample size)	3,984
Mean	82.82
Median	45.00
Standard deviation	125.27
Variance	15,693.00
Range	1361
Quartiles	25 Q1 = 12
	50 Q2 = 45
	75 Q3 = 100
Minimum	0.00
Maximum	1,361.00

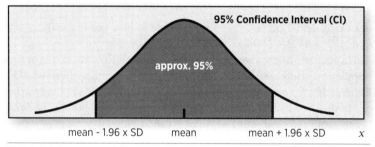

FIGURE 9.1
Normal Distribution

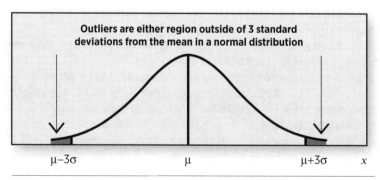

FIGURE 9.2
Outliers

A bigger standard deviation, for example 10, would indicate a bigger variation of scores around the mean.

Again, if the data are approximately normally distributed (bell-shaped; see figure 9.1), then about 95% of the data fall within the mean – 1.96 × standard deviation, and the mean + 1.96 x standard deviation. This interval (mean – 1.96 × standard deviation, mean + 1.96 × standard deviation) is called the *95% confidence interval* (CI). A person is 95% confident that a value will be between the lower end of the interval and the upper end of the interval.

For a normal distribution, any values that are either lower than three standard deviations from the mean or higher than three standard deviations from the mean are considered outliers (see figure 9.2), as discussed earlier.

So a standard deviation of 125 would imply that 5% of the libraries would have fewer than zero audiobooks; in other words, the population probably not normally distributed—or that a few libraries have extremely large audiobook collections (i.e., they are outliers), or that the person responding to the survey made a typo.

10

Matching Data Analytic Methods to Data

Table 10.1 summarizes matching a research goal with an appropriate statistical technique and characteristics of the variables. Details about each statistical technique follow in chart order.

REPRESENTATIVE RESEARCH GOALS AND APPROPRIATE STATISTICAL TECHNIQUES

Research goal: Find the direction and strength of the
linear relationship between two quantitative variables.

Technique: Pearson correlation

For example, to see the relationship between two variables, say number of library visitors and number of reference questions, where both of the variables are quantitative, then an appropriate statistical technique would be a Pearson correlation. A correlation coefficient measures how much two variables tend to change together. The coefficient is made up of both the strength and the direction of the relationship. This statistical method measures the linear association between the two quantitative variables. The range of possible

TABLE 10.1

Matching Research Goals with Statistical Techniques

Research goal	Number of variables	Types of variables	Response variable	Appropriate technique(s)	Nonparametric alternative
Find the direction and strength of the linear relationship between two quantitative variables	Two	Quantitative variables	None	Pearson correlation	Spearman correlation
Find the strength of the relationship between two qualitative variables	Two	Qualitative variables	None	Pearson's chi-square test in a contingency table	
Determine if there is a statistical difference between means of two quantitative variables	Two	Quantitative	One	t-test	One-sample sign test
Determine which levels of a factor are significantly different after determining that at least two are different (comparing means across one factor with several levels)	One with more than two levels	Qualitative	Quantitative	One-Way Analysis of Variance (ANOVA) as well as follow-up comparison tests (Two-way ANOVA is used for two factors)	Kruskal-Wallis, or could use the Mood's Median test (Friedman's Test is an alternative to two-way ANOVA)
Compare two population means where the two populations can be paired (example before/after, pre-test/post-test)	Two	Quantitative	None	Paired-sample t-test	Wilcoxon signed-rank test
When the response variable is a quantitative measure, determine which and to what extent, significant variables predict the response variable	One or more predictor variables	Predictor variables can be both quantitative and qualitative	Quantitative	Multiple regression or decision tree	
When the response variable is a categorical variable, determine what, if any, significant variables help classify the response variable	One or more predictor variables	Predictor variables can be both quantitative and qualitative	Qualitative	Logistic regression or decision tree	
When there is no response variable, group the observations into a specific number of groups and characterize those groups	More than one variable	Variables can be quantitative or qualitative	No response variable used	Clustering to find cluster groups then decision trees or regression (multiple or logistic depending on response variable) to describe groups	
Reduce the dimension of many predictor variables by grouping together those that are similar	All variables (more than one) are Predictor variables	Variables are quantitative	No response variable used	Principle components	
Measure a process over time to see if there are aspects out of control	One variable	Variable is quantitative	No response variable	Control chart	

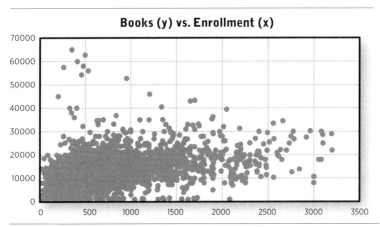

FIGURE 10.1
Scatterplot of Books versus Enrollment

values for the correlation is between -1 and 1. A value of -1 is a perfect negative association between variableA and variableB. This means that as variableA increases in value, variableB decreases in value proportionally. A value of -1 is a perfect positive association between variableA and variableB. In the real world, no two variables are perfectly related. A correlation of 0, similar to 1 and -1, is an extreme example, but this represents the case where there is absolutely no relation between variableA and variableB; it is strictly random. A correlation value of about 0.6 or higher tends to indicate a strong positive relationship between two variables. A correlation value of about -0.6 and lower tends to indicate a strong negative relationship between two variables. A correlation value around 0 (around between -0.3 and 0.3) indicates a very week association between two variables. A value between about 0.3 and 0.6 tends to indicate a moderate relationship between variables. Finally, a correlation value between -0.3 and -0.6 tends to indicate a moderate negative association between variables. An example of a strong correlation would be, for example, the library budget and the number of books. That is, as the budget goes up, the number of books would increase (or for smaller budgets, the number of books would be smaller). A negative correlation between quantitative variables may be that as the number of ebooks in the library collection increases, the number of print books borrowed decreases. It is important to point out that the Pearson correlation involves a linear relationship between two quantitative variables, that is, a change in one variable is associated with a proportional change in another variable.

An example of the Pearson correlation coefficient for enrollment versus books is 0.392. This is to be expected, as the enrollment of the school increases, the number of books is hopefully likely to increase.

The scatterplot of enrollment versus books is as follows, Pearson correlation = 0.392 (figure 10.1):

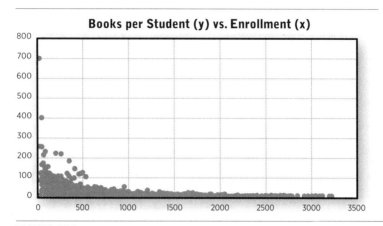

FIGURE 10.2
Scatterplot of Books per Student

However, a look at the Pearson correlation between enrollment versus books per student shows that the coefficient is moderately negative at -0.399 (figure 10.2). Thus, for bigger schools, the number of books per student actually tends to be less, which is also not surprising.

■ ■ ■ ■ ■

Research goal: Find the strength of the relationship between two qualitative variables.

Technique: Pearson's chi-square test (commonly called just the *chi-square test*) in a contingency table.

Suppose the project team wants to investigate the relationship between two variables that are qualitative (categorical), such as job title and preferred type of materials checked out. The appropriate statistical technique would not be a Pearson correlation analysis, but rather a chi-square test analysis. Each variable, in what is called a *contingency table,* would have categories or levels. An example of a chi-square test would be school level (elementary, middle, high school) versus AASL member (yes, no), as illustrated in table 10.2. A chi-square test would be used to find out if the strength of the association between the two variables is significant, or is likely to just have occurred by chance and has little value or interest to the project team.

- Null hypothesis H_0: the two variables are not related (independent)
- Alternative hypothesis H_1: the two variables are related (dependent)

TABLE 10.2

Chi-Square Test: Contingency Table

			SCHOOL LEVEL				
			Elementary	Middle	High	Other	Total
AASL member	No	Count	1,225	529	621	109	2,484
		Percentage within AASL	49.3%	21.3%	25.0%	4.4%	100.0%
		Percentage within school level	66.2%	63.9%	58.1%	46.0%	62.3%
	Yes	Count	626	299	447	128	1,500
		Percentage within AASL	41.7%	19.9%	29.8%	8.5%	100.0%
		Percentage within school level	33.8%	36.1%	41.9%	54.0%	37.7%
Total		Count	1,851	828	1,068	237	3,984
		Percentage within AASL	46.5%	20.8%	26.8%	5.9%	100.0%
		Percentage within school level	100.0%	100.0%	100.0%	100.0%	100.0%

Pearson's chi-square test, $x^2 = 47.461$; *p*-value = 0.000. Because the *p*-value = 0.000 < 0.05, this is a significant result meaning that the null hypothesis is rejected, and that the alternative hypothesis, that school level and AASL membership are significantly related, is accepted; in this case primary school librarians are more likely to be AASL members, and middle school librarians are least like to be AASL members. If the expected number for a particular cell is small (less than 5), then collapse the cells. Also, to correct for small sample size, for 2 × 2 contingency tables, the Fisher's exact test yields a more precise result.

▀ ▀ ▀ ▀ ▀

Research goal: Determine if there is a statistical difference between means of two quantitative variables.

Technique: *t*-test.

What if one variable is qualitative and one variable is quantitative? A correlation or a chi-square test is not appropriate. What about comparing librarians

TABLE 10.3

t-Test

	GROUP STATISTICS				
	AASL member	N	Mean	Standard deviation	Standard error mean
Hours per teacher librarian	No	2,484	27.826	16.3636	.3283
	Yes	1,500	29.720	14.9707	.3865

$t = -3.653$; df = 3,982; p-value = 0.000.

by whether they were AASL members or not (yes or no, i.e., categorical) and how many hours per week they worked (quantitative). A *t*-test would be used to compare the mean (average) of hours worked by school librarians who are AASL members to the mean for those school librarians that are not AASL members. That is, the user can test to see if there is a statistical difference between the average number of hours worked per AASL school librarian and the number of hours worked by non-AASL member librarians. There are two hypotheses.

- H_0: the population mean for the number of hours worked by AASL member school librarians is approximately equal to the work hours of non-AASL member librarians (i.e., H_0: μAASL = μnonAASL)
- H_1: the population mean for the number of hours worked by AASL member school librarians is NOT equal to the work hours of non-AASL member librarians (i.e., H_1: μAASL ≠ μnonAASL)

In addition to testing for a difference, it is also possible to test to see if the number of hours worked by AASL member school librarians is greater than those of non-AASL member librarians.

The following test (table 10.3) shows that AASL members average 29.720 hours per week versus 27.826 hours for non-AASL librarians. This is a significant difference (p-value < 0.05) with the p-value = 0.000. This means that the chance of getting a difference this big or bigger is extremely unlikely to have occurred by chance, and there is a high probability (more than 99.999% likelihood) of a difference existing in the population between AASL members and nonmembers in terms of the number of hours worked weekly.

■ ■ ■ ■ ■

Research goal: Determine which levels of a factor are significantly different after determining that at least two factors are different (comparing means across one factor with several levels).

Technique: One Way Analysis of Variance (ANOVA) as well as follow-up comparison tests.

TABLE 10.4

ANOVA for Student Spending

	Sum of squares	df	Mean square	f	Significance
Between groups	15363.673	3	5121.224	22.764	.000
Within groups	895371.887	3,980	224.968		
Total	910735.559	3,983			

Suppose the project team is interested in comparing a quantitative variable, books per student, versus a qualitative categorical variable (e.g., elementary, middle, high school). There are categories of one factor (school level) where the team would be comparing means (not just two categories of one factor, as in the previous example). So, the team cannot use a *t*-test; they would have to use an analysis of variance (ANOVA) to compare the three levels of means (averages).

Consequently, the output of a one-way ANOVA reveals that the overall *F*-test statistic of 22.764 (below) is significant (*p*-value < 0.05) *p*-value = 0.000 (table 10.4). This statistic means that at least one of the categories (elementary, middle, high, other) is significantly different from another group in terms of the mean number of books per student.

Then, because at least one of the groups is significant from another, individual comparisons, called *post-hoc tests,* are analyzed to find out which groups are significantly different from others. There are six possible comparisons out of the four school levels (elementary to middle, elementary to high, elementary to other, middle to high, middle to other, and high to other). A few different comparison types of tests, such as the Tukey, Fisher, Dunnet, and Bonferroni, help to make conclusions. The researcher is mainly looking to see if the overall conclusions are similar across tests. If the results show this, the researcher can state them confidently. If the conclusions from the various comparison tests are different, then it is harder to feel as confident in analyzing the results, but at least if more tests show a similar result, it is common to go with the majority findings.

Looking at table 10.5, the Tukey HSD, Fisher's least significant difference (LSD), and Bonferroni–Dunn show similar results. When comparing middle to elementary in the Tukey HSD test, the result is not significant (*p*-value = 0.915, which is greater than 0.05). However, elementary schools have significantly fewer books per student on average than high schools (about 1.8 books less per student and *p*-value = 0.009 < 0.05). Elementary students also have significantly fewer books per student than students in "Other" schools (7.8 fewer books per student). Furthermore, the Tukey HSD indicates that middle schools have significantly fewer books per student than high schools (2.2 fewer books per student) as well as significantly fewer than "Other" schools (8.3). Finally, high school students have significantly fewer books per student

TABLE 10.5

Books per Student Differences across Class Levels

	School level (I)	School level (J)	Mean difference (I−J)	Significance
Tukey HSD	Elementary	Middle	.409	.915
		High	-1.816˙	.009
		Other	-7.881˙	.000
	Middle	Elementary	-.4095	.915
		High	-2.225˙	.007
		Other	-8.290˙	.000
	High	Elementary	1.816˙	.009
		Middle	2.225˙	.007
		Other	-6.065˙	.000
	Other	Elementary	7.881˙	.000
		Middle	8.290˙	.000
		High	6.065˙	.000

than "Other" schools (by 6.1 books per student). Using LSD and Bonferroni statistical comparisons of means for those six comparisons results in the same five coming out as significant differences. The Dunnet test is done when there is a control group, which does not apply in this case. If testing several different new classes at the library to an existing class, this would be an example where the existing class would be the control level, and Dunnet's comparison test would be used to measure the impact of the intervention.

■ ■ ■ ■ ■

> *Research goal*: Compare two population means where the two populations can be paired (example before/after, pre-test/post-test).

> *Technique*: Paired-sample *t*-test.

Suppose that at the beginning of the year students are given an objective test on how well they are able to access library reference resources. Sometime after the test, the students have a class lesson in the library about reference resources. After the class, the students take the same test to see how proficient they are in their library reference skills. Each student then has two scores on the test (quantitative values): one before the library class was taken and one after the class was taken. A paired-sample *t*-test can be done to see if the class was useful in increasing the scores of the students on their library skills because it was the same student who took both exams, which makes the paired-sample t-test appropriate.

It is possible to test to see if there is a statistical average difference between the post-class score and the pre-test score for the students. If statistics show a p-value less than 0.05, then this indicates a significant increase in scores and thus the library class is shown to be useful. If the p-value is greater than 0.05 then the class is not showing any significant improvement. Consequently, there are two hypotheses:

- H_0: difference = 0 (mean of post class score—pre-class score = 0)
- H_1: difference > 0 (mean of post class score—pre-class score > 0)

In addition to testing for an increase in scores, a researcher could test to see if the H_1 difference is less than 0, which would indicate a decrease in reference test score. Alternatively, if the H_1 difference is not equal to 0, which would indicate no difference in scores between the pre-class score and the post test score. The null hypothesis, H_0, would stay the same, but the alternative hypothesis, H_1, would change (difference < 0 or difference ≠ 0). Typically, the researcher would decide on H_1 if the class had a positive effect on the scores. Alternatively, in teaching catalogers about RDA, the alternative hypothesis H_1 would be to check to see if there is an average *decrease* in cataloging practice after the class (difference < 0).

■ ■ ■ ■ ■

Research goal: When the response variable is a quantitative measure, determine which, and to what extent, significant variables predict the response variable.

Technique: Multiple regression.

Suppose the project team wants to find out what are the significant attributes that can predict total expenditures for libraries are. A multiple regression statistic would be appropriate because the response (or dependent) variable is continuous. The independent (or predictor) variables is the other variable used to determine which variables help predict total expenditures.

First, look at the F-test in the ANOVA table to see if any of the predictor variables are significant. Because the p-value associated with the F statistic (311.704) is less than 0.05, there is a significant result. That is, at least one of the predictor variables is significantly different from 0 (see table 10.6).

- H_0: all the predictor variables are not significantly different from 0.
- H_1: at least one predictor variable is significantly different from 0.

Next, because at least one predictor variable is significant, the researcher can continue developing the model (group of independent variables used to

TABLE 10.6
ANOVA *F*-Test

	Model	Sum of squares	df	Mean square	F	Significance
			ANOVA			
	Regression	268737038558	34	7904030545	311.704	.000*
	Residual	100035383161	3,945	25357511		
	Total	368772421720	3,979			

TABLE 10.7
Predictor Variable Model Summary

Model	r	r-square	Adjusted r-square	Standard error of the estimate
1	.854	.729	.726	5,035.624

predict the dependent variable). Otherwise, an additional predictor variable would be added to the model. The model can explain from 0% to 100% of the variation in the response variable, in this case total expenditures. The model of predictor variables used to predict total expenditures explains 0.726 or 72.6% of the variation in total expenditures. This can be found in the adjusted *r*-square number, 72.6%, which is a rather high number and indicates a pretty good model with a group of predictor variables that help explain the response variable total expenditures (see table 10.7).

There are some other assumptions to consider when building a multiple regression model. Are the predictors (independent variables) highly correlated with each other? How do individual variables correlate collectively with more than one other predictor variable in the model? For that, look at the column in the output labelled "VIF," or variance inflation factor. If any VIF for a particular variable is 10 or higher, look more closely at that variable to decide whether to remove that variable or, alternatively, to group that variable with similar variables. In the output shown in table 10.8, all of the VIF values are below 10, so there is not a correlation problem with the predictor variables. In addition, the difference between an estimate for each combination of predictor values in an observation and the corresponding actual response value must be normally distributed and have a mean of 0 and a constant variance (spread of data). These checks can get rather involved and complicated, but are important because the results are based on having the data follow certain assumptions. Nonetheless, several of the regression assumptions are somewhat robust (i.e., the assumptions can be broken to a certain extent and still yield reliable results).

Next, look at the predictor (independent) variables in the model to see which ones are significant. The values under significance that have an asterisk (*) are the significant variables. The variables on these rows with p-values less than 0.05 are significant variables, meaning these predictor variable coefficients are not equal to 0 and are important to the model in predicting total expenditures. The significant variables shown in the table, in addition to the intercept or constant term, are enrollment, number of teacher librarians, hours per other staff, books per student, periodicals, audios, copyright year, number of individual visits per week, spending per student, number of teachers, number of librarians 2cat, Title I school, Level=elementary, Region=Northeast, total_number_staff_3cats=0, total_number_staff_3cats=at least 2, and total computers.

The next step in the interpretation is to look at the unstandardized Coefficients B column. For the predictor variable, Enrollment, the B value is 6.300. This means that for every additional increase in one unit of enrollment, holding all other predictor variables constant (an important aspect about regression), the total expenditure increases by $6.30. If the B were a negative value, say -6.300, the interpretation would be the same, except instead of increases in the total expenditure by a certain number of units, the expenditures would be decreasing by 6.3 units (i.e., $6.30) for each additional unit increase in enrollment, again holding all the other predictor variables constant.

Enrollment was a continuous predictor variable. How would a categorical predictor variable be interpreted? Title 1 school has two levels. A school is either a Title 1 school or it is not. The significance level for this variable is 0.037. Because the significance level, the p-value is less than 0.05, it is significant. Then the interpretation for this variable is that holding all the other predictor variables constant, changing from a non-Title 1 school to a Title 1 school, the total expenditures decrease by -1,281.058 units (over $1,000 loss). The variable Level=elementary represents either elementary schools or not elementary schools. Holding all the other predictor variables constant, changing the school level from elementary to high school (the reference school) increases the total expenditures by approximately 909.69 units (i.e., $909). The categorical variables are listed as 0 or 1. Here the variable level has four types of schools. It is necessary to have one less binary categorical variable than the number of levels for a particular category. So, there are three binary variables that need to be formed from the original one variable that has four levels. The three dummy variables in this example are named Level=elementary, Level=middle, Level=other. There has to be one level held out as a reference category. In this example, high school is set as the reference category. The other two levels, Level=middle and Level=other are not significantly different than high school in this model.

There are many other predictor variables in the model, but table 10.8 shows only a few of them to demonstrate the values.

TABLE 10.8

Multiple Regression

Model	UNSTANDARDIZED COEFFICIENTS		STANDARDIZED COEFFICIENTS	t	Significance	Variance Inflation Factor
	B	Standard error	Beta			
(Constant)	-52003.840	22693.814		-2.292	.022*	
Enrollment	6.300	.259	.304	24.345	.000*	2.274
Hours per librarian	-17.747	22.652	-.019	-.783	.433	8.234
Periodicals	65.673	5.354	.120	12.267	.000*	1.395
Videos	.084	.205	.004	.410	.682	1.343
Audios	3.388	.697	.044	4.861	.000*	1.198
Title I school	-1,281.058	615.354	-.018	-2.082	.037*	1.056
Level=Elementary	909.695	283.603	.047	3.208	.001*	3.140
Level=Middle	284.818	259.872	.012	1.096	.273	1.743
Level=Other	-125.220	390.231	-.003	-.321	.748	1.339
. . .	. . .	. . .	. . .	. . .	. . .	. . .
. . .	. . .	. . .	. . .	. . .	. . .	. . .
Total computers	2.809	.526	.056	5.335	.000*	1.595

■ ■ ■ ■ ■

Research goal: When the response variable is a categorical variable, determine which, if any, significant variables help classify the response variable and to what extent.

Technique: Logistic regression.

What are the significant attributes that distinguish AASL-type libraries and those that are not AASL members? A logistic regression can help identify those attributes. This technique is appropriate when the response (or dependent) variable is a categorical variable (e.g., yes or no). The independent (or predictor variables) are the other variables used to find out which ones help differentiate libraries with or without AASL members. Note that it is also possible to do a logistic regression with more than two categories for the response variable, but this is less commonly done.

The logistic regression analysis does not have as clear a number as r-square adjusted that was in the multiple regression analysis. The model assessment numbers are basically comparative numbers to other possible models, but do

TABLE 10.9

Classification Table

			PREDICTED		
			AASL member		Percentage correct
	Observed		No	Yes	
Step 1	AASL member	No	2,207	274	89.0%
		Yes	1,122	377	25.2%
	Overall percentage				64.9%

not assess the overall fit of the model by themselves. One assessment to look at is found in the classification table above. This tells us if all the observations are run using the model, how accurately that model would classify the response variable. In other words, if a library fits the model, how well can that model predict that the library would be staffed by a librarian who is an AASL member. In table 10.9, the overall classification table classifies libraries as having AASL members or non-AASL members at a 64.9% accuracy rate. The accuracy of this particular model is reasonable. However, the goal is to get as high an accuracy rate as possible, and this of course depends on the type of data being classified. Sometimes this is rather difficult because some variables are not available in the data set.

Next, in an interpretation similar to multiple regression (table 10.10), look at the coefficients of the variables to see which ones are significant in the model (i.e., significantly different than 0). Again, an asterisk is placed next to the significant predictor variables based on those that have p-value significant levels < 0.05. Here the interpretation is found looking at the Exp(B) and is discussed in terms of odds. An example of a quantitative variable that is "hours delivering instruction," which has a significance level of 0.018 (which is significantly less than 0.05). The corresponding Exp(B) for this variable is 1.009. This means that for each additional unit of instruction (hours), the library is 1.009 times more likely to be a AASL-staffed library than a non-AASL staffed library, holding all the other predictor variables constant. If we have a Exp(B) value less than 1, then there is a lower chance of being an AASL-staffed library than not having an AASL member. For example, if the Exp(B) was 0.5, then for each additional unit of the predictor variable, there would be 0.5 times as much chance of having an AASL member, holding all the other predictor variables constant. An example of a categorical variable is remote access. An interpretation of that coefficient is that a library having remote access is 1.7 times more likely to be staffed by an AASL member than a library that does not have remote access, holding all the predictor variables constant. Another

TABLE 10.10

Variables in the Equation

	B	SE	*p*-value	df	Significance	Exp(B)
Enrollment	.000	.000	.486	1	.486	1.000
Numberteacherlibrarians	.331	.178	3.482	1	.062	1.393
Hoursperteacher	.014	.012	1.425	1	.233	.986
Hoursmeetingteachers	.011	.011	1.027	1	.311	1.011
Hoursdeliveringinstruction	.009	.004	5.612	1	.018*	1.009
Hoursoverseeingbudget	.011	.006	3.022	1	.082	.989
Booksperstudent	.002	.002	1.593	1	.207	.998
Level			24.731	3	.000*	
Level(1)	.007	.106	.004	1	.950	1.007
Level(2)	.032	.122	.070	1	.792	.968
Level(3)	.717	.155	21.318	1	.000*	2.049
Remoteaccess (numlibrarians_2cat(1)	.531	.104	25.965	1	.000*	1.701
REGION			85.395	3	.000*	
REGION(1)	.070	.109	.413	1	.520	.933
REGION(2)	-.735	.094	61.495	1	.000*	.479
REGION(3)	.143	.129	1.233	1	.267	.867
Titleschool(1)	.567	.255	4.968	1	.026*	1.764
...	...	...	...	...	...	...
...	...	...	...	...	...	...
Constant	.799	9.855	.007	1	.935	2.223

way to interpret this finding is to conclude that libraries providing remote access are 70% [100%*(1.7–1)] more likely to be staffed by an AASL member than by a non-AASL member

■ ■ ■ ■ ■

Research goal: When the response variable is a categorical or a quantitative variable, determine what, if any, significant variables help to predict or classify the response variable.

Technique: Decision tree.

A decision tree is a technique that can be used as an alternative to a multiple regression or a logistic regression. Its advantage is that the profiles within the tree can be seen, such as the profiles of likely AASL-staffed libraries. In

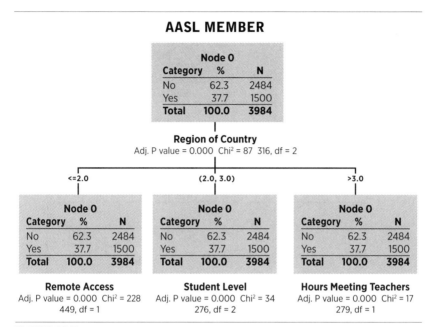

FIGURE 10.3
Decision Tree

the example above, the top box, or node, in the tree shows an overall sample with 62.3% of the libraries not staffed by AASL members and 37.7% staffed by AASL members. Going down the decision tree further separates the sample. At the bottom row of the tree (not shown) are those groups that are much different in percentages from the overall sample. For example, libraries that are in the Northeast or Midwest (coded as 1 or 2), have remote access, and have at least two staff members, have a 65.8% likelihood of having AASL members. This is much likelier than in the overall sample of 37.7%. Other profiles can be found similarly by looking at the tree. Those final nodes that have similar percentages to the overall sample of 62.3% non-AASL library members and 37.7% AASL library members do not represent important profile paths (see figure 10.3).

The decision tree classification matrix is similar to that found in a logistic regression analysis. The decision tree model shown in table 10.11 correctly classifies 63.3% of overall AASL members.

In addition to the classification matrix, the ROC curve can be used to graphically show the accuracy of a decision tree when the response variable is categorical. The greater the area above the diagonal line, the higher the accuracy. This is especially useful when multiple models are compared on the same ROC curve (figure 10.4).

TABLE 10.11
Decision Tree Classification

	PREDICTED		
Observed	No	Yes	Percentage correct
No	2,406	78	96.9%
Yes	1,386	114	7.6%
Overall percentage	95.2	4.8	63.3%

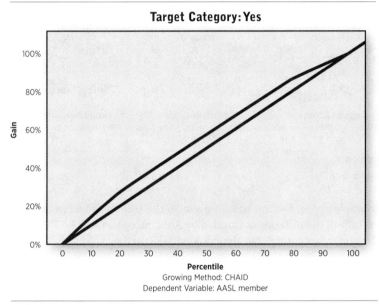

Target Category: Yes

Growing Method: CHAID
Dependent Variable: AASL member

FIGURE 10.4
ROC Chart

■ ■ ■ ■ ■

Research goal: When there is no response variable, group
    the observations into a specific number of groups and
    characterize those groups.

Technique: Clustering analysis.

If the researcher is not sure which observations group together, then she can
do a cluster analysis. A common particular cluster analysis is k-means clustering. The researcher then has to indicate to the software package how many
clusters he wants to try. So, a researcher may pick some number such as 2, 3,
or 4 to start with. Then after a cluster analysis is run, a new response variable

is discovered from the observations. For example, if two clusters are generated, then each observation will have an added response variable of 1 or 2, indicating which cluster that observation most closely identifies with. Then, a logistic regression or decision tree can be run to describe the characteristics of the two clusters. This two-step process (cluster analysis and then either logistic regression or decision tree) can be very useful in identifying groups of observations.

■ ■ ■ ■ ■

Research goal: Reduce the dimension of many predictor
variables by grouping together those that are similar.

Technique: Principle components.

If there are twenty predictor variables in a regression, there may be a problem with some of the predictor variables being highly correlated with other predictor variables (e.g., the Variance Inflation Factor (VIF) is above 10 in a multiple regression, e.g., Table X). One option is to remove predictor variables so this is no longer an issue. Another option is to use *principle component analysis*. In this technique, similar predictor variables are grouped into a single grouped variable. The 20 predictor variables could be grouped into a smaller number, for example, six principle components. Then the issue of correlated predictor variables could be drastically decreased. One issue with principle components is that the researcher may know exactly what each predictor variables could be interpreted. However, if a principle component is a grouping of, say, three variables, how is that group to be interpreted? This is left to the researcher to give a name to each component. If a component grouped hours worked by Internet staff hours, computers in library, logging of questions asked over the Internet when library is closed, maybe that group could be named "library computer component." Then this grouping of one predictor variable would take the place of the three original predictor variables in the model.

■ ■ ■ ■ ■

Research goal: Measure a process over time to see if there
are aspects out of control.

Technique: Control charts.

If measuring a variable over time (also called a *process* in quality control), control charts can be very useful to see changes across time. In a control chart, the data are plotted in time order on a chart with the average in the middle, and can have a lower limit and upper limit based on previous data. If the current data shows the variation in the process is atypical (out of control). If such points are found, the next step would be to try to understand the reasons for such unusual variation. A control chart can be useful to find ongoing processes and correcting errors as they occur. Also, a control chart can reveal

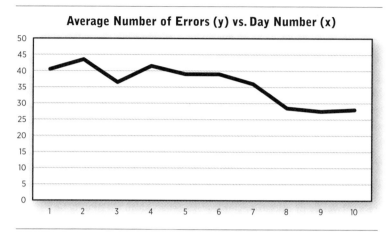

FIGURE 10.5
Run Chart of Errors over Time

fundamental shifts in a process (such as measuring errors in stacking books, and seeing a shift when new workers are starting).

Figure 10.5 is an example of a run chart. There are 10 days and each day two groups of students stack books and periodicals; their errors are counted. The average of the two groups is the middle dot. Errors were mostly above average for the first 6 days, but started to decrease after that.

NONPARAMETRIC ALTERNATIVE TECHNIQUES TO PARAMETRIC TESTS

Many tests make assumptions about distributions of the population data. For example, for a hypothesis test, an assumption is made that the data are a sample from a population that is normally distributed. Similarly, for regression, the errors are assumed to be distributed normally. For nonparametric statistical analyses, no specific population distribution is assumed.

An advantage of a parametric test is that sometimes there is increased power compared to a nonparametric test with the same sample size. Power is the probability of correctly concluding a significant result. When using nonparametric tests there is no worry about the range of assumptions needed in parametric tests. When assumptions are violated in parametric tests, the resulting conclusions may be somewhat misleading.

A decision tree analysis also does not make many assumptions and is a form of a nonparametric test, but is more commonly considered part of data mining (big data), because many observations are necessary to best be able to run the analysis. An important aspect of data mining is that instead of the assumptions associated with parametric analysis, splitting the data set into at least two randomly split parts and forming a model on one part and then testing it out on the other part (holdout sample) makes it possible to check to see how accurate the model is on "new" data.

In addition to variables that are quantitative or categorical, there are also some variables that are called *ordinal*. These variables have a rank order. For example, for a horse race with five horses, the position of the five horses at the end of the race is: first, second, third, fourth, and fifth. However, the distance between values is not necessarily equal. One possibility is that the time between first and second place could be just a few seconds, and the time between second and third place could be a minute. However, if the numbers signified the minutes to run the race, it is shown that the 2 minutes is 1 minute faster than 1 minute. Having ordinal, or ranked, data provides less information than quantitative data, but more information than categorical data. Similar to those other types of data, certain types of analyses can be done on ordinal type data.

Nonparametric Alternative to the One-Sample *t*-Test

Instead of using the parametric one-sample *t*-test to compare means, a researcher can use the analogous nonparametric one-Sample Sign test. Medians are compared, and a confidence interval of likely values of the median can also be determined.

- H_0: median = hypothesized median
- H_1: median ≠ hypothesized median

Note the not equal (≠) in H_1 can also be replaced by a greater than sign (>) or less than sign (<) depending on the goal of the researcher.

Nonparametric Alternative to the Paired-Sample *t*-Test

The Wilcoxon signed-rank test can be used when the researcher cannot assume that the population of dependent samples comes from normal distributions. This test assesses whether the population mean ranks differ for a paired difference test. The test statistic is based on the ranks of the differences, not the differences themselves.

Nonparametric Alternative to the Two-Sample *t*-Test

The Wilcoxon Mann-Whitney test is used to test the equality of two population medians. It is assumed that the data are independent random samples from two populations with similar distributions, with data that are at least ordinal.

- H_0: median population 1 = median population 2
- H_1: median population 1 ≠ median population 2

Note that the ≠ in H_1 can also be > or < depending on the goal of the researcher.

For multiple samples, the researcher could use the Kruskal-Wallis or the Mood's Median test, which offers a nonparametric alternative to the one-way analysis of variance. The Median test and the Kruskal-Wallis test look for differences among the populations' medians. For ordered categories on Y (such as low-, medium-, and high-budget), the researcher could use ordinal regression.

Nonparametric Alternative to the Pearson Correlation *t*-Test

Another correlation that measures numerical variable relationships is the Spearman rank-order correlation (also just called the *Spearman correlation*). This correlation evaluates the monotonic relationship between two quantitative variables. In a monotonic relationship, the variables tend to change together, but not necessarily at a constant rate. The Spearman correlation coefficient is based on the ranked values for each variable as opposed to the actual raw data. The Spearman correlation is often used to evaluate relationships involving ordinal variables. For example, a Spearman correlation can be used to evaluate whether the rank order in which library employees complete a number of tasks is related to the number of months they have been employed.

It is always important to graph the two variables, typically as a scatterplot, before drawing conclusions from a correlation. Just because there is a very weak correlation does not mean that the two variables are not related. Correlation coefficients only measure linear (Pearson) or monotonic (Spearman) relationships. Other relationships, as previously described, are possible. For example, consider the relationship between the amount of rain in a region and the height of corn. The correlation would show something around 0, which would indicate to many people that there was no relationship. However, this just means that the relationship is not linear (a straight line connecting the points). The relationship would be a parabola, or upside down U-shape. So, with little rain, the corn would not grow much; with a moderate amount of rain, the corn would grow well; and with too much rain, the corn would get flooded and not grow.

Variables that may be the main reason behind a correlation are called *confounding variables*. For example, suppose that a high positive correlation exists between the number of schools and crime within a specific geographic area. This may not indicate a relationship between those two variables, but rather the increased number of schools may indicate higher population, which is the reason for increased amount of crime.

11

Statistical and Survey Software for Libraries

There are many available software packages that may be useful to help achieve research goals. Almost everybody already has Microsoft Office, which includes Excel. Because there is no extra cost involved to get this software, Microsoft Excel is a viable option. However, there are many superior software packages that are more directed to data analysis than Excel. Some of the common choices are Minitab, SPSS, SAS, R, and Tableau. In addition, a couple of library-centric survey tools facilitate data collection, analysis, and visualization.

STATISTICS PACKAGES

Minitab is probably the best choice in terms of low cost and ease of use. The spreadsheet-like interface for the data (similar to Excel's) allows for easy data entry. Also, it is possible to copy and paste a data set into the spreadsheet or convert an Excel, text, or comma-delimited file into a Minitab file very easily. In addition, most of the functions are available in a pull-down menu. In addition, the graphs on Minitab look very professional, are easily labeled, and can be customized according to personal preference. Finally, if a user needs to create a program to do data analysis, that ability is available. It can create a *macro,* which is a group of commands in one function usually taking in particular input from the user. An alternative is to write a Minitab batch file, which is a list of commands that are run together so that the user does not need to use pull-down menus one at a time. In terms of data analytics, Minitab is one of the main software packages available for quality control and running Six Sigma analyses. Minitab was originally created by Pennsylvania State University in 1972, and has been updated many times since then to what is now a very comprehensive package. Minitab runs only in a Windows environment.

Another very popular statistical software package is IBM SPSS Statistics Software (which costs substantially more than Minitab). Like Minitab, it offers a very easy-to-use spreadsheet-like data interface with pull-down menu commands as well as macro/batch file capability. It has fewer advanced quality control and Six Sigma commands compared to Minitab. However, it does have some more advanced statistical options including decision trees and other analyses. One final and noteworthy advantage of SPSS is its variable view, which supplements the data view that it and Minitab offer. The variable view in SPSS is different than a regular data view/spreadsheet view in that the user can add labels to the variables as well as assign values for labels. For example, if you have 1,2,3,4 as the values for region, in SPSS they can be coded in the variable view so that 1 is used for "Northwest," 2 for "Midwest," 3 for "South," and 4 for "West" to show the character values in output. Also, variable values can be used for missing values. For example, if we put in the missing value for number of librarians as 99, then the program would automatically know that any time there were 99 librarians, this would actually indicate a missing value. (Note that most statistics software have this capability to signal when there are missing values.) SPSS was created in 1968, and is available for Windows and Mac platforms.

SAS statistical software has both a user-friendly interface version (called Enterprise Guide) and a regular SAS programming interface. Enterprise Guide is very powerful and fairly easy to use, with a good graphing capability. A person can use the pull-down menu, the "point-and-click" approach to running analyses, or the macro/batch programming environment similar to Minitab and SPSS. The cost of Enterprise Guide is competitive with SPSS, and can take advantage of many advanced statistical analyses. The data interface is also a spreadsheet-like environment similar to Minitab and SPSS. SAS and SAS Enterprise Guide run only on Windows.

R is a statistical software program that is absolutely free. It was created in 1993 and is an implementation of an older statistical language that was known as S. It is a very powerful language that is increasingly used in many academic institutions, as well as by some corporations. However, it is not as user-friendly as Minitab or SPSS because the user has to write code or use code in a programming structure to generate output, because it lacks pull-down menus or point-and-click options available in Minitab and SPSS. (There has been an attempt to improve the interface by combining the programming code, the output, the variable list, etc., into one screen in a program called RStudio.) R's statistics are extremely powerful and cutting-edge, but the learning curve may be prohibitive for many people who are not comfortable with programming. R runs on both Windows and Mac platforms.

The program Tableau does not have the statistics capabilities of the packages discussed above. However, it is very useful for visual analytics. Excel can do basic graphics of data analysis, but Tableau is much more user friendly and extensive in its capabilities for analyzing data sets over time and space on maps. It is available on both Windows and Mac platforms.

Based on cost, statistical analysis options and ease of use if one is running computers on Windows, Minitab will be the program recommended for most libraries. However, if a great deal of inputting of survey data for analysis, or only Apple computers are available, SPSS is more user-friendly. If access to SAS Enterprise Guide is available, it would be the most powerful for Windows computers. Finally, for those with no budget at all, either Excel or R would be the best options to run on either Windows or Mac platforms.

SURVEY PACKAGES

Busy library systems appreciate ready-made, validated survey tools that they can easily administer and analyze. The most popular product is LibQUAL+, which started in 1999 as an initiative of the Association of Research Libraries (ARL). Adapting the SERVQUAL survey instrument, the project aimed to measure library effectiveness. This commercial tool measures collections, operations, staff, and library usage in terms of customer-related indicators posed as 22 questions. Libraries can add five local questions as well. Part of the service includes a report of the findings. Fees depend on several factors, including training and additional analyses.

A similar survey tool with supporting service is libPAS, a product of Counting Opinions. The survey quantitatively assesses library performance. The accompanying program, LibSat, enables libraries to measure customer satisfaction continuously through qualitative feedback questions. The survey's dimensions include satisfaction, quality, usages, importance, referral, and expectations. As with LibQUAL+, Counting Opinions enables libraries to add custom questions. In terms of products, the company tabulates summary reports, and enables Excel-format data downloads. Again, products and services are fee-based.

Several free survey tools exist. SurveyMonkey and Google Forms are the best known. SurveyMonkey enables researchers to create a limited number of questions, and basic statistical tables and raw data may be exported. Google Forms is a more free-form application. Results are recorded in exportable spreadsheet format and chart images. For more features, one must pay accordingly (exemplifying the saying "you get what you pay for"). In general, most free products do not have the features or robustness to do adequate data analysis.

PART IV

Case Studies

12

Access and Retrieval

Case Study

Organization of resources for optimum access and retrieval is a core function of libraries. Ideally, a newly acquired item should be efficiently and correctly cataloged. This will require someone to receive the item (usually in the acquisitions unit) as well as a cataloger, but it may also involve many others—a subject specialist, technical specialist or LMS consultant, license workgroup, special collections manager, or translator before going to a physical-processing person (for labeling, covering, etc.) and a shelver.

Because such a complex workflow can result in bottlenecks at several points, a value stream process map is useful to visualize the material and information flows related to the process. Typically, data are collected about time and number. Data about time may include the amount of start-up or lead time; how long is spent on work, clean-up, rework, and walk time from one station to another for each stage; and computer speed. Data about number include how many operations are involved; how many products and items are processed, and their variations; batch sizes as applicable; and the value of each process (e.g., stamping a book, adding the barcode, adding security strips, etc.). Once the process map is complete, librarians can analyze productivity and value, eliminate non-value steps and wasted or duplicative effort, and streamline remaining processes that may involve bottlenecks, outdated processes,

TABLE 12.1

Failure Analysis for Missing Books

PROBLEM	DATE (FREQUENCY OF PROBLEM)						TIME TO ID (MEAN)						RESOLVED		NOTES
													MARC field	If marked	
	M	T	W	TH	F	S	M	T	W	TH	F	S			
In-library use	2	3	4	1		1	12	9	15	5	6	5			
Being transferred (e.g., ILL)			3		4				1			3	X	6	
Missing	3	5	6	2	1	3	2	1	1	1	1	4	X	4	
Withdrawn			2												
On order	2					2	2					3	X	4	
Being cataloged	3	2	3	2		2	3	1	1	1		4	X	14	
Being processed	3	3	5	3	1	2	2	1	1	1	1	3	X	11	
Being repaired	3	5	8	2	2	4	2	1	1	1	1	4	X	18	
Being shelved	4	6	10	6	3	12	8	3	12	2	2	14			
Misshelved	8	2	4	1		1	11	7	13	5	5	3			
Miscataloged	1	2	3			1	4	2	2						
Mislabeled			1						12						
Wrong barcode				1						1					
. . .															
. . .															
. . .															

excessive exceptions, inconsistent processing, and lack of training (Campbell, 2015). It should be noted that most cataloging steps apply to all formats, but may need to interface with different products such as an URL link resolver or specialized database or repository of multimedia materials.

Because errors can occur at any of these points, a failure analysis is an important aspect of quality control and effective workflow. Such errors are most likely to be noticed when a library user cannot locate the desired item. A good first step is to collect data about unavailability: what the reason for not finding the item was, and how that problem solved (McGurr, 2007). Table 12.1 is an example of how to keep track of problems on a weekly basis at the service desks. Several rows are left open for staff to identify other possible problems; once the recording has stabilized, the table can be reviewed to add possible often-reoccurring problems.

Even a cursory look at the above data reveals several patterns. It takes shelvers considerable time to determine in-library use, even more than mis-shelving. Is the time well spent in this endeavor, or should staff suggest to the requester to look around him- or herself, or check back in an hour? Data also show that the shelvers for Monday, Wednesday, and weekend take longer to find the desired item; follow-up observation and interviews can determine if the shelver is less productive or else needs training (the fact that the weekend person takes a long time to find how that the item is being shelved might point to a time-management issue). The fact that it takes 12 minutes to note that an item is mislabeled, but that it occurs just once, may illustrate that although mislabeling seldom occurs, it can significantly cost time when it does happen. Patterns emerge about why local notes are made in the MARC record; this is apparently done consistently for cataloging and repairs, but not for processing, which calls for further investigation (and might require a reminder to that unit to record their work more consistently). The relatively high number of items being repaired might also signal further investigation: What is causing the need for repairs? Are some staff over-identifying the need for repairs? Could some minor repairs such as fixing a slight tear be done at the circulation desk? Is the turnaround time for repairs reasonable? It also appears that the Monday and weekend service staff take longer to identify a problem, so their supervisor can determine the cause and develop an intervention to improve their efficiency. These data should also take into account the total circulation figures; if the daily checkout is over a thousand, then the unavailability figures are reasonable; if the daily checkout is less than a hundred, serious follow-up is needed. Some of these problems may be hard to identify, or take considerable time to figure out, which is all the more reason to identify frequent problems and resolve their causes so as to provide better service. It is obvious that collecting such data regularly can inform operations, and facilitate their targeted improvement.

Considering the data table in more detail, one of the time-savers included in the table is notation in the catalog record. While it may take 30 seconds to add (and delete) a local note in the catalog, it helps in tracking workflow (and signaling a need to address a recurrent problem), and it minimizes the time spent at the service desks—and improves customer satisfaction. The need to add such local processing notes will depend on the acquisition workload volume, cataloging procedures (e.g., at what point in the acquisitions and processing functions is a record generated), and problems in locating the item—another data analysis opportunity.

Several of these problems require someone physically look for the item; this is usually a shelver, because the service desk needs constant supervision

TABLE 12.2

Shelver Action

Date	Shelver	Number of minutes for shelver to respond	Number of minutes for shelver to locate item	Problem	Notes
2/1	Adam	3	7	Misshelved	
2/1	Cara	2	13	Mislabeled	
2/2	Raj	11	6	Misshelved	
2/3	Cara	5	2	Being shelved	

by other staff. The amount of time involved in paging a shelver, and how long it takes that person to locate the desired item, can involve considerable time—and skill. A supplementary table (as shown in table 12.2) can record such data.

The data shown in table 12.2 illustrate that locating a mislabeled item takes significant time. The data also point out that it takes Raj a long time to respond, so that delay can be investigated to find out why (e.g., is he on a break or a trip to the restroom, or just slow to respond?). That one occurrence also highlights the need to collect data regularly for an extended time period in order to determine patterns of behavior rather than jumping to conclusions because of one incident.

REFERENCES

Campbell, E., et al. (2015). Managing the e-resource ecosystem: Creating a process for sustainable e-resource life cycle workflow analysis and oversight. ACRL conference proceedings, Portland, OR, March 6–8.

McGurr, M. (2007). Improving the flow of materials in a cataloging department. *Library Resources & Technical Services, 52*(2), 54–60.

13

Benchmarking Library Standards

Case Study

Many state library systems and organizations have developed standards for libraries, but these are seldom date-driven. Because standards can be used to benchmark library effectiveness, providing ones that are data-based legitimizes such benchmarking efforts.

When the California State Department of Education and the California School Library Association (CSLA) developed model school-library standards, they wanted to make sure that school libraries would have the capacity to support student information and digital literacy success. To that end, Farmer and Safer (2010) conducted a literature review to identify variables that correlated positively to library program effectiveness, especially in terms of student learning. Some of these variables emerged consistently in the literature:

Staffing: *full-time credentialed school librarian, full-time paraprofessional*

Access: *flexible access to the library throughout the day for groups and individuals*

Services: *instruction, collaboration, reading guidance and promotion, reference, interlibrary loan*

Resources: large current diverse and relevant materials that are well organized

Technology: *Internet connectivity, online databases, online library catalog, library web portal*

Management variables: budget, *administrative support, documented policies and procedures, strategic plan with assessment)*

Based on the literature review, the research and standards committee identified those variables italicized above as the basis for the California school library baseline standards.

To develop reasonable quantitative standards to complement the baseline standards, Farmer and Safer then wanted to determine if there existed a significant difference between those school libraries that met those baseline standards and those that did not. Using the state's school library survey data set at that time, they applied descriptive statistics to identify standard variables; to be so designated, at least half of the survey respondents had to meet that specific baseline standard variable (i.e., the library didn't have to meet all of the standards).

Next, the researchers divided the data set into two groups: one that met all baseline standards, and one that did not meet all baseline standards. A *t*-test determined that the two groups were significantly different relative to resource and service standards; the most significant difference relative to the baseline standards was the presence of a full-time school librarian.

A follow-up logistic regression analysis determined the relative significance of the baseline variables, using a sideways process to generate the best model, meaning that individual variables were added and subtracted to determine their relative significance. The analysis revealed that several variables related to resources and services further differentiated the two groups: number of subscription databases, library web portal presence, information literacy instruction, Internet instruction, flexible scheduling, planning with teachers, book and non-book budget size, and currency of collection (table 13.1).

Those libraries meeting all of these significant variables were examined in terms of their material and fiscal resources. The mean value for budget, collection size, and currency became the basis for the state quantitative standards for school libraries. With these data-based standards, school libraries now have a robust assessment tool to benchmark their programs.

TABLE 13.1

Significant Variables for High-Quality School Library Programs

California variable	*B*	SE	Wald	df	Significance	Exp(B)
2+ Databases	.957	.157	37.133	1	.000	2.603
Internet instruction	1.666	.283	34.612	1	.000	5.292
Flexible scheduling	.195	.096	4.090	1	.043	1.215
Information literacy instruction	.632	.157	16.145	1	.000	1.881
Library portal	.404	.185	4.776	1	.029	1.497
Planning with teachers	.757	.143	27.900	1	.000	2.132

(*B* = coefficient; SE = standard error; Wald = test statistics; df = degrees of freedom; Sig. = significance; Exp(B) = odds ratio).

REFERENCE

Farmer, L., & Safer, A. (2010). Developing California school library media program standards. *School Library Media Research, 13.* www.ala.org/aasl/sites/ala.org.aasl/files/content/aaslpubsandjournals/slr/v0113/SLR_DevelopingCalifornia_V13.pdf.

14

Data Sets

Case Study

Storage and access to data sets have gained considerable value recently, particularly because of the emphasis of data mining. Federally funded researchers are now required to submit a plan for data set long-term management, so more institutions are creating repositories or joining consortia who manage data sets. Because of their information-science expertise, librarians are often called upon to establish these repositories. In addition, maintaining the repository facilitates librarians' collaboration with research faculty.

Deciding to add this service is not easy, especially because accepting this responsibility requires a lifetime commitment to maintenance for the life cycle of the data. Goben and Raszewski (2015, p. 41) list life cycle stages and associated decision points:

Identifying: available data, possible linked data, target and potential audience

Digitizing: current format, data integrity and stability

Cleaning: personnel handling the data, standardization rules and tools

Describing: ontology, project directions

> **Storing and preserving:** means of access, storage options, preservation duration
>
> **Sharing:** intellectual property rights, privacy, security, resource sharing
>
> **Analyzing:** analysis tools, data set limitations

Librarians need to identify current functions and workflow to ascertain the library's capacity to add a repository service. What added staffing and resources will be needed? What costs will be incurred, and how will they be remunerated? A capacity analysis should be conducted before committing to this long-term service. At the same time, librarians should also analyze the costs (and savings) of joining a data set coalition.

One of the first considerations when deciding whether to create a repository is to calculate its potential costs. The 2002 SPARC guide divides expenses into these categories: labor, software, hardware, network, and institutional overhead (Crow, 2002). Technical service costs may vary depending on if the work is done in-house or outsourced, but in either case, the quality and capacity of work may be the chief factor. Non-technical staff usually outweigh technical staff, particularly in terms of administration as well as resources processing.

The platform itself has several underlying costs. Even an open source solution such as Prints and DSpace may incur technology support costs; although these two products offer off-the-shelf implementation they have the capability to be customized for local needs and linked to other products. Productivity database applications such as Access and FileMakerPro require more upfront planning and design, and are not suitable for large collections. Turn-key solutions may cost more, and if they have unneeded features, then the product could be underused for the cost associated with it. Data analysis can help with the decision as each criterion is identified and weighted, along with total cost and unit cost.

Even if the library has a repository, how the materials are added needs to be evaluated for efficiencies. For example, the library might have the faculty input the data sets and assign the field information for themselves, which saves the librarian time. However, the quality of inputting might be uneven, with the result being that data sets are hard to retrieve. One impact of such uneven quality may be that the reference desk spends 10% of their time helping users retrieve the data sets. Therefore, the library might consider asking the researchers to provide the library with the data sets, and then a librarian would do the processing (e.g., input the fields). Alternatively, the library might have a librarian review each new inputted data set to clean up and standardize the data set record. The question is, does the library have the capacity to have librarians process the data sets, or should it continue to have the faculty

TABLE 14.1

Repository Labor Impact

	Salary per hour	Number of database transactions per week	Number of hours per database transaction	Total cost per week
Reference librarian (retrieve database record)	25	30	.3	$225
Database librarian (clean up data record)	30	10	.1	$30

TABLE 14.2

Assumed Cost Analysis after Two Years

	Add a repository service	Do *not* add a repository service
Labor over 2 years	$15,000	$22,500
Existing data set records processed	All 5,000 records	No previous records
Total cost	Savings of $7,500 over 2 years and all previous data set records processed	

produce the draft data set record, and merely hire a library staff to clean up the drafts (see table 14.1).

Obviously, the library would save money if the data set record were reviewed and cleaned from the start. The question becomes, does the library have the capacity for a database librarian to clean up all the existing data set records? If the library has a collection of 5,000 records, it would take the database librarian 500 hours to clean up the entire repository, at a cost of $15,000. If the database person spent 40 hours per week (which would be her total function), it would take 12.5 weeks. The database librarian, however, does have other work to do, and her supervisor says that only 15% of the work week can be dedicated to this task, which converts to 4 hours. In 6 hours, the database librarian can clean up 60 data set records per week (10 new ones and 50 existing ones). Therefore, it would take her 100 weeks (2 years with 2 weeks' vacation per year), as shown in table 14.2.

The conclusion will answer the question of whether to add a repository service to the library; the cost analysis shows us that by adding a repository service, we reduce costs over a two-year span by $7,500 and have processed all the existing data set records. So, it makes sense to add a repository service.

REFERENCES

Crow, R. (2002). *SPARC institutional repository checklist & resource guide.* Washington, DC: SPARC. www.sparc.arl.org/sites/default/files/IR_Guide_%26_Checklist _v1_0.pdf.

Goben, A., & Raszewski, R. (2015). The data life cycle applied to our own data. *Journal of the Medical Library Association, 103*(1), 40–44.

15

Digitization

Case Study

Digitization of resource materials has become a mainstay function of libraries for several reasons: to preserve information archived in deteriorating formats, to increase functionality (such as examining documents in fine detail), to expand access to resources, to conserve physical space, to secure master documents, to generate output to other media, and to maintain material that was originally recorded in digital form that might be inaccessible due to changing software and hardware.

However, the process of digitization can be labor-intensive, time-consuming, and require specialized technology and training (Boock, 2008). The Association of Research Libraries (2004) developed standards and best practices for digital reformatting (Arthur, et al., 2004). They follow two frameworks: the Open Archival Information System Reference Model ISO 14721:2003, and the OCLC/RLG Preservation Metadata and the IASL Information Model framework.

Digitization involves several steps.

1. *Pre-scanning*. Make sure the item has not already been digitized. Check for bibliographic integrity (completeness and legibility). Check intellectual property rights, and manage permissions.

2. *Image capture and quality control.* Ensure that hardware and software meet technical targets for high quality and faithful capture. Orient, sequence, and name each object, page, and image to reflect the resource's original presentation. Choose a format and interface based on the nature of the original resources and its expected use.

3. *File format.* Save digital files in a standards-based format, and record data to describe the format.

4. *Production of web-accessible files.* Scan files. Incorporate optical character recognition as appropriate. Ensure that file formats are accessible from web browsers, and include standard encoding schemas.

5. *Metadata.* Provide standards-based metadata to describe the resource, give contextual information, guide page and image-level navigation, and indicate special features such as indexes.

6. *Digital preservation.* Refresh files by moving them to new storage periodically. Check for the integrity of the digital file (e.g., completeness, corruption). Keep more than one copy, and compare copies for data integrity. Migrate files to new formats to ensure continued compatibility and access. Emulate files by enabling obsolete systems to run on newer systems.

Bottlenecks and failures can occur within and between each step, so the workflow as a whole, each step, and the transition between steps can be analyzed for efficiency and quality control. Figure 15.1 (Garcia-Spitz, 2010, p. 10) shows that different library units at the University of California San Diego Library share the digitization work: Mandeville Special Collection Library, Digital Library Program, Metadata Analysis and Specification Unit, Information Technology Development.

At each step, the process needs to be documented in order to ensure that all documents are digitized correctly. A table of document records may include the following data: physical or folder name, document number, file name, pixel dimensions, device source, other technical information, and time.

Note that the flowchart, while time sequenced, does not include units of time. Such calculations are useful to ascertain the cost per item. For example,

10,000 images × 5 minutes/image to enter and export data = 1,200 hours = 30 weeks (40 hours/week).

1,200 hours × $15/hour = $18,000

Therefore, the labor cost for the one process is $1.80/item, not counting the cost of the technology. The flowchart can facilitate the overall digitizing cost and cost per item.

It should also be noted that digitizing costs begin even before routine digitization processing. The library needs to acquire and install hardware and

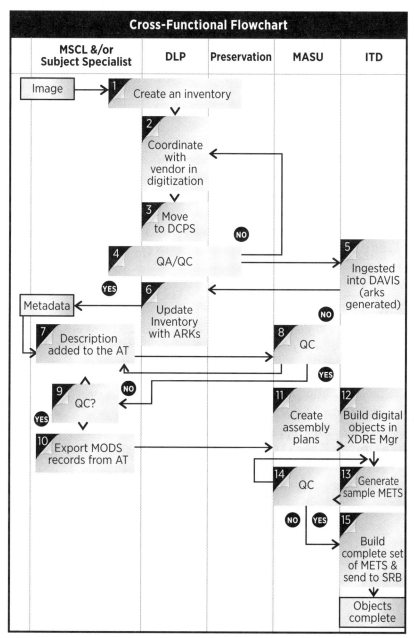

FIGURE 15.1

Digitization Cross-Functional Flowchart

software for digitizing and storage, design web pages for digital collections, set up the facilities for digitizing, train all staff involved in digitizing, and develop policies for digitizing efforts such as selecting and prioritizing resources to be digitized.

One way to prioritize items to digitize is to calculate their relative importance based on agreed-upon criteria. Boock and Chau (2007) expressed expected project performance (P) as $((2*IS) + ES + Uniq + Exp) *100$ where IS = internal stakeholders, ES = external stakeholders, Uniq = content uniqueness, Exp = public exposure and recognition; each criterion is rated on a 5-point scale. Then P is divided by total cost in thousands of dollars to derive the relative value. For example,

$$2 * 3(IS) + 4(ES) + 1(Uniq) + 4(Exp) * 100 = 1500(P) / 25(C) = 60(V).$$

REFERENCES

Arthur, K., Byrne, S., Long, E., Montori, C., & Nadler, J. (2004). *Recognizing digitization as a preservation reformatting method*. Washington, DC: Association of Research Libraries.

Boock, M. (2008). Organizing for digitization at Oregon State University: A case study and comparison with ARL libraries. *Journal of Academic Librarianship*, 34(5), 445–451.

Boock, M., & Chau, M. (2007). The use of value engineering in the evaluation and selection of digitization projects. *Evidence Based Library and Information Practice*, 2(3), 78–86.

Garcia-Spitz, C. (2010). Applying MPLP to digitization: A project manager's perspective. Western Roundup Conference, Seattle, April 28–30.

16

Ebook Collection Development

Case Study

ncreasingly, libraries subscribe to—or acquire—electronic books (ebooks). At first glance, ebooks offer an attractive alternative to physical books in regard to timeliness of information (especially in fast-moving industries such as computer science and medicine), increased access (especially for distance users), reduced processing costs (e.g., physical processing labor costs, supplies cost), reduced space costs, reduced maintenance costs (e.g., filing, damage, security, loss), greater user convenience, format preference and customization (e.g., font size and style), and accessibility for individuals with special needs.

On the other hand, librarians complain about licensing agreements and limitations, packaging or bundling of titles (similar to database aggregators or jobber bundling of print titles), digital processing and cataloging, access constraints, lack of platform standardization, low usage, the need to review contracts annually (and loss of documents if not renewed), which raise questions about ebook cost-benefit.

To help make this decision, librarians can create a balanced scorecard that clarifies various perspectives, as shown in table 16.1. It should be noted that perspectives may well overlap, which can facilitate negotiation and stakeholder buy-in (Pickett, Tabacaru, & Harrell, 2014).

TABLE 16.1

Balanced Scorecard

	Objectives	Measure	Targets	Initiatives
Clientele	Convenient access to needed, timely information	Fulfill rate	95% access to resources within 72 hours	Request resources
Internal Operations	Optimize collection development processes	ROI, fulfill rate, efficient workflow	Decrease cost/book 5%, save 5% turnaround acquisitions time	Compare cost/book of print and ebooks, review workflow
Financials	Optimize ROI of resources	ROI	Decrease cost/book 5%	Compare cost/book of print and ebooks
Library improvement	Optimize collection to support organization and its clientele	ROI, fulfill rate, efficient workflow, user satisfaction	Decrease cost/book 5%, 95% access to resources within 72 hours, save 5% turnaround acquisitions time	Compare cost/book of print and ebooks, review workflow

Whatever the decision, librarians need to determine which vendor to choose. However, additional criteria must be considered when selecting an ebook vendor—as featured in the matrix in table 16.2. This simple decision matrix facilitates comparisons among potential vendors. The decision group determines which criteria to consider, and their relative importance. Each person evaluates the products independently, and then averages the scores or arrives at some other way to reach a decision based on the scores.

In the above case, vendors B and C practically tie, so the decision team can eliminate vendors A and D and then determine the next steps: discussing differences in ratings, reassessing the relative weight of each criterion, contacting other users of the products, and requesting an in-depth demonstration to which the technical staff are invited. In any case, the data clarify the issues to be resolved.

Another criterion to consider when choosing an ebook vendor is the product's own data collection features. Librarians should identify collection management decision points and determine what kind of data the product should collect automatically. Table 16.3 details possible data and the use of that data.

Many libraries begin by subscribing to one specialized ebook vendor, such as one that focuses on business or medical publications. Several data points can be used to ascertain the most effective subject: number of interlibrary loan requests by major, copyright date of current holdings (particularly for subjects that change quickly), types and quantity of research assignments by

TABLE 16.2

Decision Matrix

VENDORS		A			B			C			D		
EVALUATORS		E	F	G	E	F	G	E	F	G	E	F	G
	Weight												
Subscription cost (including multi-year, multiple copies, group discount)	× 4	16	16	12	12	8	12	12	12	8	12	16	16
Quality and variety of possible titles	× 4	8	4	8	16	12	16	12	12	12	12	8	8
Acquisition basis (e.g., automatic acquisition upon X hits, micro fee per hit)	× 2	2	4	2	2	4	4	6	6	6	4	2	2
Total number of potential users versus likely number of simultaneous users	× 3	2	2	2	8	8	6	6	6	4	6	8	6
Circulation options (e.g., access time frame per session, download time frame)	× 1	2	3	2	4	4	3	4	4	4	4	3	2
Downloading and saving options (e.g., read only, download x number of pages maximum, length of time that downloaded document exists for a user)	× 1	1	1	1	3	3	4	3	2	2	2	2	3
Printing options (e.g., number of pages)	× 1	1	2	1	4	4	3	3	3	4	2	1	1
Dynamic versus static IP address access	× 2	4	4	2	6	8	8	8	8	6	4	6	6
Processing options (e.g., cataloging, linking to library management system)	× 2	2	4	4	6	8	6	8	8	8	4	6	4
Sharing and archiving options	× 1	1	1	1	3	4	4	2	2	3	3	2	1
Technical and other service options (e.g., cost, turnaround time, availability)	× 2	2	4	2	6	8	8	8	6	6	4	4	4
Training options (e.g., number of trainees, support material, level of training, frequency of training, locale, cost)	× 1	2	1	1	4	6	4	8	6	6	4	4	6
Technology requirements	× 2	8	8	6	6	6	6	8	4	6	4	4	4
Platform(s)	× 1	1	1	1	4	4	3	3	4	3	2	1	1
TOTALS		52	55	45	84	87	87	91	87	88	67	67	64
AVERAGES/MEAN		51			86			88.7			66		

TABLE 16.3

Usage Data

Usage data	Data analysis use
Number of hits per title	Possible print or digital acquisition; possible course packet/copyright issue
Number of hits per publisher	Possible print or digital acquisition
IP address	Identify repeat users, campus versus remote access, identify service points
User demographic data (by login info)	Collection management decisions (e.g., acquisition, curriculum support)
Downloading activity	Possible print or digital acquisition; possible course packet/copyright issue
Timing and length of sessions	Possible print or digital acquisition; possible course packet/copyright issue
Technical help data (e.g., frequency, type of problem)	Service and platform reconsiderations

major, requests for titles by major, clientele survey about interest and use of ebooks, and the observations of subject liaison librarians. These data points can be weighted as in the example above to determine which academic domain to target when subscribing to an ebook vendor.

Whatever decision is made, librarians have baseline data to use to compare with data gathered after a reasonable time period, such as a semester, to determine the impact of the vendor choice and acquisitions. To what extent are the balanced scorecard targets met?

It should be noted that publicity about the new acquisitions also needs to be factored into the analysis. Theoretically, the same announcements about additions to the collection can be made as for other formats. However, librarians would lose a golden opportunity if they did not advertise their new collection development direction. While it would be difficult to parse out the explicit publicity from the status quo communication, the very act of surveying the community and involving them in the decision-making already raises awareness (and possibly expectations), so librarians might have to chalk up the increased circulation to public relations. Probably the only way to determine if explicit advertising impacted circulation would be to survey those individuals who checked out an ebook.

REFERENCE

Pickett, C., Tabacaru, S., & Harrell, J. (2014). E-approval plans in research libraries. *College & Research Libraries* (March), 218–231.

17

Facilities

Case Study

The library as space remains a central concept because people search for a third or affinity space to pursue personal interests and socialize. The library's physical space also provides a unique experience for its users, which an online presence cannot duplicate. This aspect of the library comes with a price: property maintenance, renovation, and taxes; utility bills; security measures; parking nightmares; and so on. How, then, can that space be most effectively utilized? Data helps clarify these issues.

Popular data gathering methods include user surveys, focus groups, interviews, and observations. All these instruments measure stakeholders' perceptions (including observer bias). All methods except observation can capture perceptions about possible changes or ideal facilities, but need to be tampered by fiscal realities. Sometimes librarians have constituents draw pictures of current and ideal libraries as a visual way to capture perceptions. Roughneen and Innear (2015) had students take photos of favorite library areas (and an embarrassing, less favorable area).

All of these perception measures can be codified quantitatively and analyzed. Their power increases when demographic information is captured at the same time. For instance, Roughneen and Innear (2015) found that senior students preferred different areas, and used the library differently, than did freshmen students.

Another tested method is benchmarking, in which libraries compare facility space and use with similar libraries or established standards (e.g., total area, number of computers, percentage of functional spaces, etc.). These measures are usually analyzed using descriptive statistics.

Technologies can mitigate some perceptual biases. Preiser and Wang (2006) and Xia (2005) used geographic information system (GIS) tools to determine how library space is used. A floor plan indicates functional spaces, and a GIS query feature can measure frequency indexes of each space, determining the ratio of facility occupancy to total facility per functional space or floor. Temporal comparisons can also be based on such data.

Preiser and Wang (2006) also incorporated building performance evaluation (BPE) in their assessment of 41 library branches, examining levels of performance for: "1) health, safety and security; 2) functionality, efficiency and work processes; and 3) social, psychological and cultural" aspects (p. 195). Each functional space (e.g., reference area, teen area, storage space, restroom) was labelled as a variable, and each space was rated on a five-point scale in terms of lighting, noise level, temperature, odor, furnishings, accessibility, security, and attractiveness. Libraries were also identified by six quantitative indicators: service area (population and size of area), usage (circulation, hours of operation, number of programs, number of visits), building (building space, parking space, building age), site (physical quality of property), staffing (full-time equivalent staff, staff cost per circulation), and capacity (ability to accommodate non-circulation activities such as Internet, room capacity, seating, resources).

In the same study, GIS geocoding identified users (based on circulation records) by their home address; the number of active users in a census block group generated a density pattern. Those blocks where two-thirds or more of the households used the library were designated as primary areas, and blocks where between one-seventh and two-thirds of households used the library were designated as overlap areas. The primary and overlap areas combined to create an "effective service area" designation for analysis purposes. Preiser and Wang also used census data to identify the percentage of households in poverty, the availability of vehicles per household, age distribution per household, and educational attainment by household. Additional special data identified block geographical (e.g., rivers) and use (e.g., industrial versus residential) characteristics.

The four-point scoring criteria were based on national benchmarking standards and local expertise. Each indicator was also assigned a weight reflecting the relative value of each indicator. The rating scores were totaled, and those branches with high composite scores were considered high performers.

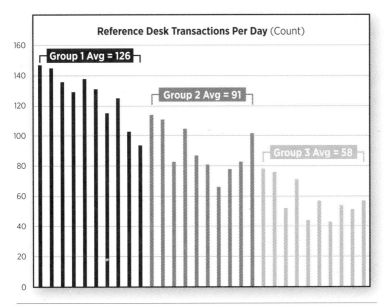

FIGURE 17.1
Representative Clustered Performance Graph

Moderate and low performers were also determined through a cluster analysis. Top performers tended to be large suburban branches that were heavily used. Moderate performers tended to be smaller buildings in more urban areas. The 10 low-performing branches served only an eighth of their service-area populations. Differences in performance levels were reflected in other ways. For instance, in top-performing branches, the average cost per circulation (i.e., circulation per full-time staff members' salaries) was 90 cents, as compared with the bottom performers where the average cost was $1.41. Moreover, only 10% of high-performing libraries had parking deficits compared with three-quarters of low performing branches. Top-performing branches had more capacity, and most low-performing branches had no meeting rooms.

The comparative data (figure 17.1) not only enabled library administrators to identify those branches that needed improvement, but also enabled them to target interventions for specific indicators for individual and groups of branches. For example, the main deficiencies in terms of facilities were found to be insufficient number of computer workstations, old or inappropriate furniture, inadequate staff work space, and inaccessibility. The data analysis resulted in generating four strategies to apply to branches: either make no major changes, upgrade or expand facilities, replace facilities, or consolidate branches with overlapping service areas.

REFERENCES

Preiser, W. E., & Wang, X. (2006). Assessing library performance with GIS and building evaluation methods. *New Library World, 107*(5/6), 193–217.

Roughneen, M., & Kinnear, J. (2015). Listen, talk, imagine: A case study of ethnography as a tool for school planning. *Independent School,* (Summer), 80–83.

18

Information Audit

Case Study

An information audit is a "process that examines how well the organization's information needs and deliverables connect to the organization's mission, goals and objectives" (St. Clair, 1997, p. 5). More specifically, it evaluates the information environment, noting what information is needed and what information is provided in order to identify and rectify possible gaps and dysfunctions. In the process, an information audit maps the information scene both within the organization and between the organization and its external environment. As the information audit data are analyzed, recommendations for strategic planning and management should emerge; typically, an information policy is generated to provide guidelines for information's effective collection and use. The audit process also helps to relate information, its uses within the organization and its context, and facilitates supportive interaction among the organization's entities. Librarians are certainly well positioned to spearhead such endeavors both within library settings as well as in other organizations.

Henczel (2001) posited a seven-stage information audit.

1. *Planning:* developing clear objectives, scope, and methods for the audit; identifying stakeholders and needed resources

2. *Data collection:* collecting and developing an information resource database

3. *Data analysis:* organizing data for analysis, and using an appropriate analytical method

4. *Data evaluation:* interpreting the data to relate with organization's information environment

5. *Communicating recommendations:* informing stakeholders

6. *Implementing recommendations*: developing a policy and plan to improve the information environment

7. *Information auditing as a continuum:* assessing the implementation's effectiveness

According to Henczal, some of the possible objectives of an information audit include: identifying key information gaps and duplication, aligning information to organizational objectives, determining the effectiveness of information-related services, mapping information workflows, and identifying clientele information needs. A successful information audit should help reduce costs, justify and improve current resources and services, support restructuring of information services, and improve the information culture.

Vo-Tran (2011) described such an information audit for an architectural firm. The firm wanted to understand the impact of information in the organization. Data collected included architectural documents, data based on observation, and anecdotal evidence based on interviews. The generated database of information resources revealed that projects are won by a tendering process; that staff work in multidisciplinary project-based teams, and may work on multiple projects depending on workload and expertise; that directors may lead up to three projects at a time; and that projects last between 6 months and 4 years. The audit revealed several information challenges: ineffective and duplicative storage of documents and images, lack of documentation stating the reason for architectural changes, need for reuse of information, and uneven transfer of project details to new staffers. This analysis of information data led to recommendations for improved information usage.

Tables 18.1 and 18.2 are samples to help codify information and its use.

TABLE 18.1

Information Audit

Resource	Task	Source	Format	Importance
Bibliographies	Information literacy instruction	Reference librarian	Web page, paper	Medium
Salary figures	Payroll	Business manager	Digital database	Critical

TABLE 18.2

SIPOC Table

Supplier	Inputs/requirements	Process	Outputs/Requirements	Customer
Vendor	Resource	Create resource metadata	MARC record	Technical service librarian
Technical service librarian	MARC record	Check MARC record with book	Corrected MARC record	
"	Corrected MARC record	Add local holdings information to MARC record	Corrected and localized MARC record	
"'	Corrected and localized MARC record	Import MARC record into integrated library management system	Modified integrated library management system database	Integrated library management system user

SIPOC table exemplifies an information workflow for the acquisition and processing of MARC records (Turner, 2015).

REFERENCES

Henczel, S. (2001). *The information audit*. Munich, Germany: K. G. Saur.

St. Clair, G. (1997). The information audit I: Defining the process. *InfoManage, 4*(6), 5–6.

Turner, A. (2015). Implementation of batch cataloging: A case study. Association of College and Research Libraries conference, Portland, Oregon, March 25–28.

Vo-Tran, H. (2011). Adding action to the information audit. *The Electronic Journal of Information Systems Evaluation [Internet], 14*(2), 167–282.

19

Instruction

Case Study

Librarians provide not only physical, but also intellectual, access to information. With respect to online information, much of which librarians cannot vet or curate, users need to be able to evaluate those resources.

Academic librarians, in particular, are picking up the instructional torch as they witness the lack of information literacy skills of incoming students and realize that their academic faculty colleagues often have not had formal training in information and digital literacy.

On the one hand, specific information literacy skills are easy to assess: can the learner locate relevant resources such as scholarly articles; what is the quality of the learner's bibliography; how critically does the user evaluate resources? On the other hand, assessing information literacy as a whole can be daunting because of its numerous aspects. In the latter situation, typical assessments include research papers and standardized multiple-choice or short-answer tests.

Measurement of information literacy competency from research paper efforts usually entails using rubrics (Scharf, 2014). Ideally, subject-domain faculty and librarians begin by identifying exemplary research papers. Then they identify those criteria that distinguish these papers, noting specific information literacy competencies, and create a rubric that can be used to assess other research papers. To calibrate assessment, the assessment team should identify at least three representative papers (high-, medium-, and low-quality) and independently assess them with the rubric. The assessors then compare their assessments, and discuss their reasoning. They should reach consensus, which might entail changing the rubric or assessing additional papers that lend themselves to easier calibration (Lockhart, 2014).

The other assessment tool, standardized testing, can be validated using quantitative item analysis. A test of information literacy is constructed with more than enough questions to address all the information literacy standards. Students then take the test as a summative evaluation. Next, an item analysis is performed to determine which test questions should be revised, deleted, or kept for future tests. The first step is to calculate an item difficulty index: the number of students who answer the question correctly divided by the total number of students. For true/false questions, the range should be 60–90%; for questions with three possible answers, the range should be 20–80%; for questions with four or more possible answers, the range should be 35–85% (Nunnally, 1972). Second, the top and bottom quartiles of students are identified based on their total test scores. The percentage of top students minus the percentage of bottom students who answer a specific question correctly becomes the discrimination index, that is, the extent to which each question contributes to the total test. A difference of at least 20 percentage points between the top and bottom groups should exist; otherwise, the question does not add much value to the test overall. Additionally, within each question, at least 5% of students should have selected each possible answer. With these indexes in hand, the assessment team can modify the test as needed.

REFERENCES

Lockhart, J. (2014). Using item analysis to evaluate the validity and reliability of an existing online information literacy skills assessment instrument. *South African Journal of Libraries and Information Science, 80*(2), 36–45.

Nunnally, J. (1972). *Educational measurement and evaluation* (2nd ed.). New York, NY: McGraw-Hill.

Scharf, D. (2014). Instruction and assessment of information literacy among STEM majors. *Integrated STEM Education Conference, IEEE,* 1–7.

20

Knowledge Management

Case Study

In this competitive society, intellectual capital has grown in value. Because companies have more fluid personnel because of economic fluctuations, they need to make sure that proprietary knowledge is shared internally, but not externally. Newcomers need to be inculcated quickly, and exiting employees need to transfer their knowledge to their successors efficiently, in order for the enterprise as a whole to keep operating smoothly between human resource transitions.

In libraries, such knowledge sharing is often organized as an in-house repository. In academia, such repositories may consist of curriculum-related resources, research and raw data sets, and internal administrative documents. In corporate settings, these repositories typically include internal documents such as plans, procedures, policies, and memos; technical specs and other documentation; and research and development documents. In most sectors, financial and personnel documents usually reside in a separate secure server.

In sum, knowledge management (KM) has become a core function in many sectors. Dalkir (2011) defined knowledge management as "the process of applying a systematic approach to the capture, structuring, management, and dissemination of knowledge throughout an organization to work faster, reuse best practices, and reduce costly rework from project to project" (p. 3). By systematically identifying, gathering, and classifying in-house publications and knowledge into a structured collection, organizations can create a system for accessing and sharing this information, and relating to their practice. KM identifies what the organization knows and does well, including tools, techniques, workflow, and strategies. Dalkir (2011) identified the following steps in knowledge management:

1. Knowledge capture
2. Acquisition of resources
3. Validation and refinement
4. Knowledge codification
5. Storage and organization
6. Presentation
7. Dissemination
8. Application
9. Assessment and value realization
10. Sustaining and divesting

This process calls upon the skill set of librarians, who know how to gather and curate information. However, for KM to be valuable to the organization, librarians must grapple with several challenges (Davenport, 2004). Librarians need to develop a deep understanding of the organization and its context in order to identify and acquire relevant information. As they describe and organize information, librarians need to code that information in a way that is meaningful to the organization. Librarians need to customize the KM interface to enable organizational members to retrieve the information intuitively and in alignment with their work. Each of these challenges requires effective collaboration between librarians and the rest of the organization.

Each of the above steps involves planning, decision-making, and monitoring, which can be optimized through data analysis. Tables 20.1 and 20.2 provide some relevant activities, performance measures, and associated data analysis methods.

Knowledge management requires much time and effort, including buy-in by employees to contribute to the repository (Critchlow, Garcia-Spitz, & Smith, 2014). Even before a collection is planned, librarians and other stakeholders need to ascertain the viability and relative benefit of an organizational system. Literature reviews, benchmarking, balanced scorecards, and impact/effort matrixes are all ways to gather data that can be analyzed to determine if repositories are cost-effective. For example, as shown in table 20.3, an impact effort matrix is a 2 × 2 grid that helps organizations assess solutions for their relative impact given the effort required. It provides a quick way to filter out

TABLE 20.1

Knowledge Management Steps

KM steps	KM performance indicators
Knowledge capture	Employee satisfaction, process capacity, process analysis
Acquisition of resources	Process capacity, process analysis
Validation and refinement (evaluate, clean, reformat)	Quality analysis, quality control, failure analysis, process capacity, process analysis, time analysis
Knowledge codification (index)	Error and tolerance analysis, process analysis, time analysis
Storage and organization (structure)	Process capacity, process analysis, quality control
Presentation (value, context)	Employee satisfaction
Dissemination (fax, print, email, etc.)	Employee satisfaction, failure analysis, process capacity, process analysis
Application	Employee satisfaction
Assessment and value realization	Employee satisfaction, job analysis, quantity analysis, quality analysis, time analysis, cost-benefit analysis
Sustaining and divesting	Quality analysis, process capacity, process analysis

TABLE 20.2

Knowledge Management Performance Indicators and Data Analysis Tools

KM performance indicators	Data analysis tools
Cost-benefit analysis / ROI	Pugh matrix, SIPOC chart
Customer satisfaction	Regression analysis, Likert techniques
Error and tolerance analysis	Pareto analysis, control chart
Failure analysis	Pareto analysis, control chart
Job analysis	Demerit systems, flow chart
Process capacity	Process capacity
Quality analysis	Pugh matrix, control chart
Quality control	Control chart, run chart
Quantity analysis	Histogram, run chart
Time analysis	Run chart, Poisson distribution, activity network diagram
Workflow/process analysis	SIPOC, fishbone diagram, activity network diagram, flow chart, run chart

TABLE 20.3
Impact Effort Matrix

	Hard to do	Easy to do
High impact	Develop in-house repository through original programming coding	Adopt existing database program
Low impact	Develop a myriad of field pull-down menus	Enable user-developed tags

solutions that might not be worth the effort. The best solutions are in the upper right quadrant—easy to implement but with substantial impact.

Part of that assessment needs to include an information audit (another case study) to identify existing documentation: its organization, use, and value. The audit can also include a discrepancy analysis to reveal what documentation is missing, or needs to be created, in order to improve operations. In many cases, procedures are learned and implemented through word-of-mouth or trial-and-error, with no archived material to support training and monitoring. The ultimate question is, "would a centralized system of documentation cost-effectively improve the organization?"

More specifically, the process for structuring a repository should be carefully analyzed in order to facilitate contributing to and accessing organizational documents. Because developing a repository from scratch is very time-consuming, librarians can jump-start efforts by first exploring existing repositories that could be used to submit documents, joining a consortium such as the Interuniversity Consortium for Political and Social Research. If security issues are paramount and an in-house solution is required, librarians can still research existing repository frameworks as listed, for instance, in the Registry of Open Access Repositories (http://roar.eprints.org). One of the most popular open access solutions, DSpace, maintains a user registry so librarians can search for repositories of similar institutions or domain-specific repositories. Librarians can develop a list of weighted criteria to assess the viability of adapting an existing repository's structure, and have stakeholders critically compare different products to help ascertain which solution would be most satisfactory.

One major aspect of repository development is the associated metadata (Hutt, Rose-Sandler, & Westbrook, 2007). If another repository is adopted or adapted, its metadata could also be used. As with the overall repository, the metadata and their structure with existing potential repositories can be assessed to determine their fit. This assessment can be done in at least three ways: (a) stakeholders can try to access relevant resources, and a failure analysis can be conducted; (b) stakeholders can try adding sample preexisting organizational documents to the targeted repository, using a failure analysis or error and tolerance analysis to measure the structural model's fit; and (c) the organization's existing inventory of documentation can be analyzed in terms of its existing metadata to ascertain to what degree the current system could be applied to a repository structure, and what changes would need to be made, or what standards adopted, for the documents to be efficiently retrievable.

Whatever repository framework is chosen, librarians need to pilot-test the inputting and retrieval processes with a representative sample of existing organizational documents. This pilot-testing needs to involve both a workflow analysis to make the process more efficient and a quality control analysis to ensure accurate performance.

Of course, the ultimate test is organizational improvement, with the repository being found to significantly contribute to its positive change. Each step along the way in its development and implementation will impact its ultimate impact.

REFERENCES

Critchlow, M., Garcia-Spitz, C., & Smith, R. (2014). *The evolution of the UC San Diego Library DAMS*. Digital Initiatives Symposium, University of San Diego, San Diego, California, April 9. http://tpot.ucsd.edu/metadata-services/mas/data-workflow.html.

Dalkir, K. (2011). *Knowledge management in theory and practice* (2nd ed.). Philadelphia, PA: Elsevier.

Davenport, E. (2004). Organizations, knowledge management and libraries: Issues, Opportunities and challenges. In H. Hobohm (Ed.), *Knowledge management: Libraries and librarians taking up the challenge* (pp. 81–90). Munich, Germany: K. G. Saur.

Hutt, A., Rose-Sandler, T., & Westbrook, B. (2007). Balancing the needs of producers and managers of digital assets through extensible metadata normalization. *Against the Grain* (Feb.), 41–43.

21

Lending Devices

Case Study

While print materials continue to be the main formats that libraries circulate, a long history of audio-visual and realia lending exists. As part of some libraries' efforts to mitigate the digital divide, they have circulated technologies, particularly portable electronic devices. However, such equipment needs special attention because parts can get lost, the device's functionality can be compromised through poor handling as well as corrupted files, and the device itself may become lost or stolen. Moreover, devices often constitute a greater financial commitment than traditional resources. Even if borrowers are careful with the device, they may need training on its use, which means that the library staff need to know how to operate the equipment and be able to explain its workings. Even with all these challenges, the process of circulating devices may be problematic when demand exceeds supply—or when little need is apparent.

Chapman and Woodbury (2012) explained how data analysis improved their libraries' device-lending program. Specifically, they wanted to identify the patterns of demand and wait time for lending items across the academic year in order to determine the lending capacity. To this end, they set up reporting logs, and surveyed them hourly and daily to monitor utilization

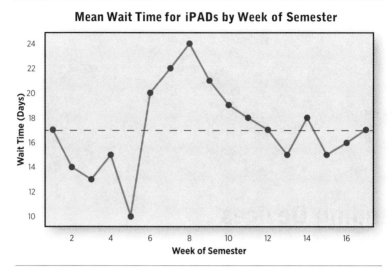

FIGURE 21.1
Control Chart

percentage as well as repair records. The reservation database was analyzed to determine wait times, which included both the time that the equipment was being used by a patron as well as the time it took to check in and process the device for possible damage and remove files that were left on the device.

A control chart that notes the waiting length over time for devices is a good way to visualize these patterns (see figure 21.1). Processing time should be recorded separately in order to determine the need to improve the task's efficiency and thoroughness (as measured by repair record).

Capacity can be measured by the number of devices that can be processed and circulated within a given time frame. If the library lends several kinds of devices, the waiting time and number of demands can be compared. If one kind of device consistently has a longer waiting period, then that data can signal the need to purchase more of those devices—or the lending period could be shortened if follow-up interviews with the borrowers find that the actual time spent using the device is significantly less than the lending period. This change in lending period increases capacity. In this case study, one ereader platform had a much longer waiting period than another ereader platform because fewer were acquired. Librarians found out that users actually did not understand the difference between the two ereaders, or that in actuality either platform was satisfactory, so the librarians improved the description of the devices, and the waiting time differential disappeared.

Data findings can determine an acceptable wait time and acceptable processing time. Then the data can be analyzed more granularly to see if patterns emerge for those devices that fall outside the acceptable range. For instance, if demand is greatest the hour before closing because the library is closed for the weekend, and users can check the devices out for a longer period, the library might need extra help the last hour to process and circulate devices. The data might reveal that check-in/processing time is longer in the evenings, when students manage the circulation desk. Observation of their work habits and interviews with staff can ascertain if the students need more training, or if they are being more thorough than other staff, so that appropriate interventions can be implemented.

In this case study, librarians found that the reservation process was counter-productive. A third of the students did not pick up the devices when they were ready (in fact, they never borrowed them), letting the equipment stay idle when it could have been used by others. The time it took library staff to monitor the reservation database, check for the returned device, contact the reserver, and label and set aside the device onto the hold area diminished the time available to check in and process returning equipment. The librarians decided to abandon the reservation function, and provide the devices on a first-come, first-serve basis, which was much more efficient.

By capturing the relevant circulation and processing data, librarians can discover significant patterns that can then be examined to determine the reasons for those patterns, and then control for those variations, thereby providing better quality, more consistent service.

REFERENCE

Chapman, J., & Woodbury, D. (2012). Leveraging quantitative data to improve a device-lending program. *Library Hi Tech, 30*(2), 210–234.

22

Marketing Virtual Reference Services

Case Study

To optimize usage of library resources and services, librarians usually need to market their programs. To this end, librarians need to identify the needs and interests of their intended clientele, and then match those wants with the library's resources and services. Particularly when libraries provide a new service, they need to market it strategically. The American Marketing Association defines it as "an organizational function and a set of processes for creating, communicating, and delivering value to customers and for managing customer relationships in ways that benefit the organization and its stakeholder" (Wood, 2010, p. 2). Strategic marketing involves finding an effective mix: choosing the right message and communications process for each targeted market segment (e.g., group of users).

New library resources and services should derive from its stakeholders' needs and wants, which in themselves can constitute marketing efforts as the library seeks to gain value in those stakeholders' eyes. Nevertheless, even the most beneficial aspects of the library may require explicit marketing in order to inform and attract users.

Virtual reference service can exemplify marketing efforts. Librarians typically add this service to their reference function for several user-based

TABLE 22.1

Data Collection Plan

Data	Instrument	Process
Number of online service hits	Library webpage count using Google Analytics	Chart daily count at 8 am
Time of service	Google Analytics	Chart daily at 8 am
User demographics	Automated user ID login OR librarian interview query	Link user ID with campus data; OR librarian codes user demographics (e.g., major, rank, local or distance learner)
User satisfaction	Post-service checkbox OR librarian interview query OR repeat usage	Add to logout process; OR derive degree of satisfaction from interview transcript; OR webpage history can record number of times that the same ID occurs (may require supplemental programming)
Source of awareness of service	Checkbox as part of login OR librarian interview query	Add to login process (may require supplemental programming); OR derive data from interview transcript

reasons: user convenience; distance education support; attraction for new users; extended service hours when the library is physically closed; greater service capacity, especially if provided in collaboration with other libraries. Despite its potential benefits, virtual reference service tends to be underutilized, which surprises librarians, who assume that they will be bombarded by online queries.

Such was the case at Texas A&M University. As with other libraries, the Texas A&M University Libraries did not market their new virtual reference service, thinking that it would be a big draw (MacDonald, vanDuinkerken, & Stephens, 2008). While some technical glitches may have negatively impacted usage, the Texas A&M University librarians decided that an explicit marketing effort was needed in order to increase virtual reference service use. They also wanted to take into account the quality of the service.

First, the librarians had to decide what data to collect and the means to collect those data. Table 22.1 summarizes the data collection plan.

The demographic data collected should include the total number of students at each rank (lower division, upper division, graduate), the total number of students and total number of faculty in each major (or college or department), and the total number of distance students as compared to the total student population. In this way, librarians will have a more informed picture about comparative use. For instance, four philosophy faculty members might use virtual reference service, and eight science faculty members might use it. However, if only 4 philosophy faculty members exist, and 40 science faculty members exist, then the relative percentages give a much more accurate picture: 100% philosophy usage compared with 20% science usage.

It is also evident that collecting data requires time and effort—and attention. Virtual reference librarians need to be trained to ask demographic, user satisfaction, and awareness questions. Moreover, someone has to review and code the transcripts to extract those data. While data that are generated automatically reduce the librarian's time, a programmer needs to spend time creating and linking the program to the existing service. The marketing planners need to consider and weigh these factors as they make their data collection plan.

Once the data collection plan and components are in place and tested, the marketing team can collect base data for a long enough period of time to establish a pattern: at least 50 hits.

The team should also collect data about the various ways that library users become aware of library services. The process could be as simple as asking users as they enter or leave the library—or in an opening pop-up box when they log onto the library website—how they find out about library services. For more nuanced information, the user could be asked the same question at each service point (e.g., reference desk, tech desk, circulation desk, librarian office). The data could be collected three hours a day (e.g., 9:00–10:00 am, 2:00–3:00 pm, and 7:00–8:00 pm) for a week. Alternatively, librarians could survey a sample number of classes (e.g., a morning, afternoon, and evening class—three each for lower division, upper division, and graduate in each department) during one week, and ask students how they become aware of library services. Users can also be asked how they would like to find out about library services (which the library might or might not use at the time). To facilitate data collection, a matrix similar to table 22.2 can be used. Technically, data could be collected on a template uploaded onto a tablet to facilitate data entry and coding.

Asking clientele about preferred communications channels can help librarians determine what existing channels need to be marketed more strongly, and which channels to add (e.g., social media).

Even at this point, data analysis can inform the marketing team. Some of the guiding questions are:

- Is there a significant difference in virtual reference service awareness by major or rank?
- Is there a significant difference in virtual reference service use by major or rank?

TABLE 22.2

Usage Data

Usage (not aware, not used, used once, used >1 time)				Major (Humanities, Arts, Education, Math/Science, Social sciences)					Rank (Lower, Upper, Grad, Faculty, STAFF)					Channel (Library website, Campus website, Signage, Peer student, Teacher, Handouts, Other)					
?	no	1	>1	H	A	E	M	S	L	U	G	F	S	L	C	S	P	T	H	O

TABLE 22.3

Overall Library Awareness and Usage

Usage	Percentage		
Not aware	64% (*n* = 5,226)		
Aware	36% (*n* = 2,922)	Aware and used	22% (*n* = 1,786)
		Aware and not used	14% (*n* = 1,136)

- Is there a significant difference in the communications channels identified?
- Is there a significant difference in the communications channels identified by major or rank?

Descriptive statistics can be used to determine the frequency, median, and mode statistics of usage and communications channels identified. Visualizing the statistics can facilitate interpretation. Splitting the data set results in more meaningful analysis. For instance, the data set can be split by types of clients: unaware, non-users, and user in order to see how different ranks and majors use the virtual reference service. Additionally, pie charts can visually capture the comparative percentage of users by major and rank, as well as by identified channels. Likewise, cross-tabs can be applied to reveal possible relationships between ranks or majors and communications identification.

Tables 22.3 and 22.4 present possible data sets and accompanying statistics to analyze.

- H_0: Major and Awareness are not related
- H_1: Major and Awareness are related

p-value = 0.028 < 0.05 so one would reject the null hypothesis, H_0, and conclude the alternative hypothesis, H_1. That is, major and awareness are related.

TABLE 22.4

Library Awareness and Usage by Major

	Aware	Unaware	All
Humanities	1,050 33.8%	2,060 66.2%	3,110
Arts	700 36.6%	1,211 63.4%	1,911
Education	412 36.9%	705 63.1%	1,117
Math/science	200 39.2%	310 60.8%	510
Social sciences	560 37.3%	940 62.7%	1,500
All	2,922 35.9%	5,226 64.1%	8,148

Pearson chi-square = 10.866, df = 4, p-value = 0.028.

The table shows that people from math/science and the social sciences tend to be more aware of the new library services than those in the humanities.

Among just those people on campus who are aware the service exists (2,922), 1,786 people have not used the new library services and 1,136 have used the new library services (table 22.5). Is there a difference among rank amongst those who are aware of the services?

- H_0: Rank and Usage are not related
- H_1: Rank and Usage are related

(p-value < 0.001) < 0.05 so one would reject the null hypothesis, H_0, and conclude the alternative hypothesis: H_1. That is, rank and usage are related. The table shows that undergrads who are aware of the new library services are using the services at a much lower rate than others on campus who are aware of the new library services.

Librarians should discuss these findings with discipline faculty, and might also ask faculty to share their syllabi to determine if assignments exist that are likely to need some reference help (e.g., research papers and annotated bibliographies). For instance, the history department is likely to assign more research papers than the math faculty, so reference usage should differ accordingly; if virtual reference service is dramatically lower than expected, then it would be a reasonable conclusion to focus on that underserved population. Librarians might also want to focus on entering freshman, because of their lower usage so that they would be more likely to have more opportunities to use virtual reference than seniors.

TABLE 22.5

Library Awareness and Usage by Rank

Rank	Aware and not used services	Aware and used services	All
Lower	1283 77.1%	380 22.9%	1663
Upper	314 41.2%	449 58.9%	763
Grad	102 29.8%	240 70.2%	342
Faculty	39 39.8%	59 60.2%	98
Staff	48 85.7%	8 14.3%	56
All	1786 61.1%	1136 38.9%	2922

Pearson chi-square = 481.796, df = 4, p-value = < 0.001.

Based on this analysis, the marketing team can make some decisions. They can increase the frequency of some communications channels with targeted market segments—in this case, freshmen. Librarians can also combine that finding with the data showing that lower division students are most likely to become aware of virtual reference service from their instructors. Librarians might well decide to visit required freshmen English classes to publicize virtual reference service. The following month, the marketing team can reassess the virtual reference data to determine the effectiveness of the added targeted effort.

Existing communications channels probably will not sufficiently increase in virtual reference use to satisfy librarians. They are likely to determine that more communications channels are needed. Ideally, the marketing team should try out one additional communications method that they think would have potential, such as a banner ad on the library website. In that way, librarians can control for the one change. Of course, librarians realize that reference requests vary by time of year, so it is best if they have the prior year's data about virtual reference use as a benchmark. In the worst-case scenario, librarians can compare the relative number of reference interactions online versus face-to-face in any one given time period.

An alternative marketing strategy is a campaign approach for which several communications channels are used simultaneously to reinforce the message (e.g., posters, announcement on the library's public access computer screensaver, presentation at student orientation, campus email blast, etc.). This approach is more difficult to measure in terms of the impact of each channel, because users might not be aware which strategy caught their attention first.

REFERENCES

MacDonald, K. I., vanDuinkerken, W., & Stephens, J. (2008). It's all in the marketing: The impact of a virtual reference marketing campaign at Texas A&M University. *Reference and User Services Quarterly, 47*(4), 375–385.

Wood, M. (2010). *The marketing plan handbook* (4th ed.). Englewood Cliffs, NJ: Prentice Hall.

23

Optimizing Online Use

Case Study

Collecting data about library clientele's online use can inform decisions about collection development and its use, instruction, and other potential value-added services such as supporting faculty research. Certainly now, as more people seek information online, libraries need to market online resources that they own, access, or create.

Libraries routinely gather data about the access and use of subscription database aggregators: vendor, specific database, journal, and article, as well as abstract versus full-text access, saving and downloading actions, and time-stamping patterns. These data can lead to decisions about vendor and database selection and specific license agreements about usage basis and access to specialized features.

Usually the easiest data to collect about web page use is URL hits, using tools like Google Analytics. If the library has a social media presence (e.g., LinkedIn), such services often have a premium level that includes data analytics features. Sometimes IP addresses are captured in the process, but the raw data is seldom disclosed; instead, country-level statistics are likely to be provided, which are seldom useful for most libraries. On the other hand, some member-based social media sites allow "likes" and links, which can identify individuals; however, it takes a great deal of effort to generalize users by demographic characteristics such as age, gender, ethnicity, or institutional status.

Another useful Internet-connectivity tool is a workstation's web history. The specific machine can capture web lookups and download histories per session. Technically, such data can be maintained on a server, although the amount of data generated can be overwhelming. In most cases, librarians can get an adequate idea of online behavior by randomly looking at computer monitor screens, web histories, and printer histories.

Parsing user online behavior by demographics is very useful in that librarians can then do targeted marketing and instruction. For instance, if freshmen seldom use subscription databases, then librarians can work with faculty teaching freshmen courses to highlight the benefits of those databases—and how to use them efficiently. If veteran employees or administrators request help only by email and not by the library's online form or digital reference service, then a demo during a staff meeting might be useful. As noted in the discussion about virtual reference service, getting personal data can be problematic for two reasons: technically linking that data set to the library's server data, and insuring some sense of privacy and confidentiality. Both educational institutions and vendors must comply with stricter rules about data use. Fortunately, for internal assessment purposes, such data collection is less security-conscious, and it is often easier to scrub local data.

To gather more in-depth online behavior data, librarians can identify a representative sample of users such as two or three females and two or three males at different educational or employee levels, also taking into account other demographic data as appropriate (e.g., ZIP code, age range, ethnicity, academic achievement). The sample population can then be asked to do think-aloud procedures in finding information and resources online; this method is called *conversation analysis*. The librarian can take field notes and ask for clarification as each person states his or her steps and thinking processing.

This method is particularly valuable when testing the interface or accessibility of a library website; librarians can also provide alternative page layout, and ask the participant to navigate through the page and say which layout is preferred and why; a task protocol created ahead of time ensures consistent wording and data capture (Jantz, 2003; Tidal, 2015). Conducting such think-alouds with five or six varied testers usually suffices to generate user patterns.

Increasingly, librarians are using screencasting applications to collect detailed data about online behavior. Simple free tools such as Jing enable users to record screen actions and voice-over think-aloud narrations for up to 5 minutes, which is usually enough time to get an idea of how an individual seeks information. Other benefits of this data collection technique include privacy (the participant can search without anyone looking on), convenience (the participant could potentially do the process anywhere anytime), and savings in staff time (because they do not have to sit with the participant). Automatic programs such as XKeyscore are able to mine interactive key action too.

While these think-alouds generate rich data, their value lies in the organization and analysis of those data. Typical factors to code include: total session time; time frame for each action; time frame per screen; part of the screen viewed; scrolling action; link and page sequencing; key words used; fields used (such as author, title, subject); searching strategies (such as use of Boolean operators, delimiters); search modifications; and zero-hit outcomes. These data can identify searching bottlenecks and efficiencies that can inform targeted instruction and advice. Data can also be divided into novice and expert searchers, enabling librarians to create a predictive model about effective searching strategies.

REFERENCES

Jantz, R. (2003). Information retrieval in domain-specific databases: an analysis to improve the user interface of the alcohol studies database. *College and Research Libraries, 64*(3), 229–39.

Tidal, J. (2015, March). One site to rule them all: Usability testing of a responsively designed library website. *Association of College and Research Libraries conference proceedings,* Portland, 593–604.

24

Reference Staffing Patterns

Case Study

By far, the largest expense item in library budgets is salaries. Therefore, the cost-effective allocation of human resources demands careful consideration, which data analysis can facilitate.

What level of education and expertise is needed to do the job? Measures of performance include quantity of work, quality of work, degree of autonomy (because supervision time can be expensive), productivity (use of time), user satisfaction, and cost-effectiveness (i.e., cost per unit of work divided by the salary). In some cases, in-house training of a paraprofessional, particularly for routine tasks, is more cost-effective than hiring a professional for the job. In some libraries, information and reference services, or technical help desks, are tiered, so that easier or more typical questions are handled by paraprofessionals, and more complex issues are referred to professionals or specialists.

Similarly, how should personnel be allocated? Is it more cost-effective to have one person do all collection development, and another person do all instruction, or are subject specialists who manage both resources and services a more effective model of resource allocation? To what extent is cross-training effective? Should librarians be generalists or specialists (e.g., children's services or business specialist)? Again, data analysis of performance measures can clear up the picture.

Reference and information service are ripe for staff discussion. At what point should more than one person manage the reference desk: the length of a queue, the time of day, or specific weeks in a semester? Is it more effective to have a call button or to email text to summons a reference person rather than have that person sit at the desk all the time? Should reference librarians roam, or stay at the desk? What hours of reference service make sense? What are the implications if staff does other work at the reference desk, such as creating bibliographies; does that activity deter users from asking for help—and does that divided attention negatively impact staff productivity? These questions can daunt administration, but data analysis can facilitate decision-making.

Archambault (2012) analyzed reference transaction data, which was inputted using the Gimlet question tracking system. To get word counts, she employed the Simple Concordance Program (http://textworld.edu/scp/). A random sample of transactions were analyzed using SPSS to generate frequencies, relationships, and standardized residuals. Some of the findings follow.

> Among directional questions, the topics of technology, library materials, and library building constituted three-quarters of the total (each of the topics receiving about a quarter of the queries). Drilling down each of those three topics by word frequency revealed that a third of building questions dealt with the location of a specific room. Therefore, librarians created PowerPoint slides for frequent directional questions, which were displayed as a loop slide show at the reference desk and directional signs for restrooms (addressing a frequent query) were posted. Online FAQ pages and clickable tag clouds handled other frequent questions such as borrowing procedures. Two-thirds of technology questions focused on the availability of a scanner and a color printer, so those items were purchased and made highly visible. Printing questions were also frequent, so a desktop screen saver image explained ways to prevent and deal with printing problems.

> The data included users' majors (see table 24.1), so cross-tab analysis revealed that business majors asked more difficult questions (as measured by length of time to answer the question, and five-point degree of difficulty) than other majors; business majors also used reference services more on Mondays and Tuesdays than other days. Therefore, the business librarian staffs the information desk on Mondays, and piloted a satellite roving reference service at the School of Business on Tuesdays (and checked virtual reference queries at that time).

TABLE 24.1

Reference Transactions by Major

Length of time to answer question	Business major	Non-Business major	Total
Low	187 45.4%	930 51.4%	1,117 50.3%
High	225 54.6%	881 48.7%	1,106 49.8%
All	412	1,811	2,223

Pearson chi-square = 4.776, df = 1, p-value = 0.029.

The transactions also captured data about which specific databases were queried, so a frequency count generated a list of those titles used more than five times. Librarians then developed workshops to teach clientele how to use each of the most queried databases.

54.61% of all business majors asked questions that took a high amount of time to address, as opposed to only 48.7% of nonbusiness majors. This is significant at the $p = 0.029$ level which is significant ($p < 0.05$).

As a result of the data analysis, fewer directional questions were asked, and the number of questions about computer availability and rebooting dropped. Traditional reference question rate has remained steady since the change.

Murgai (2006) also analyzed reference transactions by time and day, applying a chi-square statistical test to determine if significant differences of query load by time. If a significant difference existed, then standardized residuals of greater than or equal to two needed to be examined to identify major contributions, such as staff allocation changes. Of the 80 hours examined, 29 hours were identified as positive contributors to reference workload; as a result of the data analysis, additional staff were added 11:00 am to 1:00 pm Mondays through Thursdays. Table 24.2 exemplifies this process.

Similarly, Peters (2015) described how his library analyzed reference transactions to determine cost-effective reference desk staffing, especially in light of decreased number of reference questions. The two key data variables analyzed were: (a) the total number of reference desk queries, and (b) the percentage of those queries that required professional expertise to answer them. The library also maintained a gate count; that number decreased 8.8%, as compared to 48.8% decrease of reference service help for the same period of time. The percentage of questions requiring professional expertise fell from 32.2 to 26.2% over four years' time. Data analysis of the transactions also captured peak time usage. Another data point was printing. A library-specific

TABLE 24.2
Reference Transactions Totals

Time	Monday	Tuesday	Wednesday	Thursday	Friday	All
9–10	23	19	12	20	4	78
10–11	59	49	57	50	20	235
11–12	62	58	49	61	31	261
12–1	71	68	65	73	39	316
1–2	68	56	59	63	41	287
2–3	41	34	30	39	23	167
3–4	43	34	32	39	14	162
4–5	31	22	19	29	2	103
ALL	398	340	323	374	174	1,609

Pearson chi-square = 26.807, df = 28, p-value = 0.529, so there is not a significant relationship between time and day of the week.

printing process required constant attention from the reference desk staff. When a new, standardized printing system was installed, printing questions dropped by 40%, and the responsibility for printer maintenance and trouble-shooting was transferred to the access services department, which meant one less reference desk task. As a result of triangulating the data findings, library administration assigned a paraprofessional for peak reference times, and complex questions were referred to the professional librarians on an on-call basis (one in 30 questions). On the other hand, the number of higher-level reference consultations in librarians' offices rose 50% to 329 per year, and bibliographic instruction sessions rose about 10% to 289 annually. The release time from the reference desk for professional librarians gave them more time to prepare for instruction and consultations.

REFERENCES

Archambault, S. (2012). Desk statistics under a microscope = improved library services. IFLA conference, Helsinki, June 11–17.

Murgai, S. (2006). Staffing needs of the reference desk at the University of Tennessee at Chattanooga: A statistical approach. *Public Services Quarterly, 2*(2–3), 167–190.

Peters, T. (2015). Taking librarians off the desk: One library changes its reference desk staffing model. *Performance Measurement and Metrics, 16*(1), 18–27.

25

True Costs of Acquisitions

Case Study with Implications for Selection Practice

ow much does a book cost? Librarians confront this issue when a patron pays for a lost or damaged item. Usually the library charges the replacement fee (i.e., how much the item now costs rather than how much it cost in the first place), and may tack on a handling fee. Some librarians apply a blanket standard fee that reflects the average labor and supplies costs for acquiring and processing an item. However, the total cost of acquisitions may be deceptive.

A good model for calculating the total cost of acquisition is TDABC: time-driven activity-based costing (Kaplan & Anderson, 2004). The steps are as follows:

1. Identify the groups/departments involved in the process (here, adding a book).
2. Estimate the total cost of each group (salaries, materials, overhead).
3. Estimate the practical capacity of each group (e.g., total work hours, not counting meetings, vacations).
4. Calculate the unit cost of each group (i.e., total group cost divided by capacity).

TABLE 25.1

Total Cost of Acquisitions

	Total cost	Hours	Unit cost	Time/unit	Cost/event
Select item	200,000	5,250	38.10	.3 hours	11.43
Process request	200,000	5,250	38.10	.08 hours	3.05
Place order	200,000	5,250	38.10	.03 hours	1.14
Process invoice	40,000	1,750	22.86	.15 hours	3.43
Receive item	40,000	1,750	22.86	.01 hours	0.23
Reconcile item with order and invoice	40,000	1,750	22.86	.03 hours	0.69
Catalog:	100,000	3,500	28.57		
Update holdings				.02 hours	0.57
Import record				.04 hours	1.14
Copy catalog				.06 hours	1.71
Original catalog				.2 hours	5.71
Cover	70,000	3,500	20.00	.06 hours	1.20
Label and barcode	20,000	1,750	11.43	.03 hours	0.34
Stamp	20,000	1,750	11.43	.01 hours	0.11
Secure (strip)	70,000	3,500	20.00	.02 hours	0.40
Shelve	60,000	5,250	11.43	.02 hours	0.23
TOTAL UNIT COST					$12.82–17.96

5. Determine the estimated time for each event (e.g., place an order, catalog one book).

6. Multiply the unit cost of each group by the event's estimated time.

Table 25.1 illustrates how this model is applied to calculate the total cost of acquisition of printed books. Note that supplies are subsumed in the total cost.

The figures represent typical lengths of time, but do not take into account extra time needed when, for instance, items do not match the shipping list, or when imported records have errors that have to be rectified. The data also do not reflect the relative percentage of items that need to be cataloged in different ways; technical services would need to collect that data in order to refine the total cost of acquisition, as follows:

Of 1,000 items:

Update holdings:	15% × $0.57 = $28.50
Import record:	63% × 1.14 = 718.20
Copy catalog:	13% × 1.71 = 222.30
Original catalog:	9% × 5.71 = 513.90
TOTAL CATALOGING COST:	$1,482.90
	for an average of $1.48/unit

Added to the chart above, the average total cost of acquisition per title is $13.73. Nor does this cost include the time to announce the new acquisition or get back to the requester about fulfilling the request. With these figures, one could safely assign the figure of $15 for handling costs for a print book, on top of the cost of the book itself. To be sure, replacing a book usually entails just updating the holdings, but if the exact same edition cannot be procured, then additional cataloging will be required.

Having these data also helps calculate the cost of acquiring an ebook. The processing and shelving costs are eliminated ($2.28/item), but the time to select and negotiate the licensing agreement and the need to review and renew that agreement each year may well offset the processing costs. The specific calculations can be generated using the same method as shown above, and analyzed accordingly. If the costs are found to have no significant difference, then the choice to add ebooks should be based on criteria other than cost, such as circulation statistics and user satisfaction. Data for such criteria can then be collected and analyzed (Downey et al., 2014).

On the other hand, the data above reveal that the greatest cost (83%) is the selection process, which involves locating and reading reviews, comparing possible titles, and locating the vendor (which in itself can be analyzed in terms of comparing vendors). While replacing a book does not require identifying the title, the time to locate the relevant item or its equivalent, and searching for a vendor who can supply that item, can be a time-consuming effort. Again, the specific calculations can be generated using the same method as shown above, and analyzed accordingly.

The cost of selection raises the issue of demand-driven acquisitions. When the library acquires an item based on a request, the selection process is eliminated or reduced, depending on the library's policy (the library might automatically order the item, or it might still require a librarian to locate reviews and ascertain the quality of the request). If the library keeps track of the basis for item acquisition (e.g., request, librarian selection, blanket order), and matches those items with their circulation record, then a decision about demand-driven acquisition can be data-driven. Table 25.2 illustrates this issue.

TABLE 25.2

Basis for Acquisitions

Basis for acquisition	Number of titles	Average number of circulations	Standard deviations
Request	350	1.2	.6
Blanket order	100	.8	.7
Librarian selected	175	.6	.4

TABLE 25.3

ANOVA Table

Source of variation	Sum of squares	df	Variance	F	p
Between groups	45.36	2	22.68	44.47	0.00
Within groups	317.19	622	0.51		
Total	362.55	624			

An ANOVA statistic is applied to see if a significant difference exists among the three bases for acquisition (table 25.3). Finer grained data can reveal possible significant differences at the domain level (Fischer et al., 2012).

TUKEY HSD POST-HOC TEST

Request versus blanket order: $p = 0.0000$ * significant

Request versus librarian selected: $p = 0.0000$ * significant

Blanket order versus librarian selected: $p = 0.0662$ NOT significant

There is a significant difference between means for request and blanket order, between request and librarian selected, but not between blanket order and librarian selected.

All other factors being equal, one could make a good case for relying mainly on demand-driven acquisition. With their specialized training in selection, librarians might balk at such a decision. The question becomes, why are some items circulated more than others, especially when comparing requests to librarian selection? Faculty requesters might require students to use the material, and student requests might foster peer recommendations and ensuing borrowing. Librarians could conduct focus groups to follow up on materials that were acquired through requests to ascertain the basis for such items' choice and circulation. In this way, librarians can discover requester's selection and use patterns, including publicity about resources, which can inform librarians' own selection practices.

This situation also reveals the conundrum of the tension between quality and popularity, with which librarians have to grapple. At least, that tension can be examined based on data. If the underlying issue is awareness, then librarians can use this opportunity to showcase professional reviews and high-quality materials added to the library's collection. After such action, librarians can gather circulation data over the next month to see if circulation figures change, which might indicate that such communication is an effective practice. Likewise, librarians can also examine the quality of the ensuing requested resources to determine if they have more positive reviews than former requested items. In either case, these data help librarians in their collection development and promotion efforts.

REFERENCES

Downey, K., Zhang, Y., Urbano, C., & Klingler, T. (2014). Print book vs. DDA ebook acquisition and use at KSU Library. *Technical Services Quarterly* 31(2), 139–160.

Fischer, K., et al. (2012). Give 'em what they want: A one-year study of unmediated patron-driven acquisition of ebooks. *College and Research Libraries, 73*(5), 469–492.

Kaplan, R., & Anderson, S. (2004). Time-driving activity-based costing. *Harvard Business Review, 82*(11), 131–138, 150.

Bibliography

Archambault, S. (2012). Desk statistics under a microscope = improved library services. IFLA conference, Helsinki, June 11–17.

Arthur, K., Byrne, S., Long, E., Montori, C., & Nadler, J. (2004). *Recognizing digitization as a preservation reformatting method.* Washington, DC: Association of Research Libraries.

Boock, M. (2008). Organizing for digitization at Oregon State University: A case study and comparison with ARL libraries. *Journal of Academic Librarianship, 34*(5), 445–451.

Boock, M., & Chau, M. (2007). The use of value engineering in the evaluation and selection of digitization projects. *Evidence Based Library and Information Practice, 2*(3), 78–86.

Brassard, M., Finn, L., Ginn, D., & Ritter, D. (2002). *The Six Sigma memory jogger II.* Salem, NH: GOAL/QPC.

Campbell, E., et al. (2015). Managing the e-resource ecosystem: Creating a process for sustainable e-resource life cycle workflow analysis and oversight. *ACRL conference proceedings,* Portland OR, March 6–8.

Chapman, J., & Woodbury, D. (2012). Leveraging quantitative data to improve a device-lending program. *Library Hi Tech, 30*(2), 210–234.

Critchlow, M., Garcia-Spitz, C., & Smith, R. (2014). *The evolution of the UC San Diego Library DAMS.* Digital Initiatives Symposium, University of San Diego, San Diego, California, April 9. http://tpot.ucsd.edu/metadata-services/mas/data-workflow.html.

Dalkir, K. (2011). *Knowledge management in theory and practice* (2nd ed.). Philadelphia, PA: Elsevier.

Davenport, E. (2004). Organizations, knowledge management and libraries: Issues, opportunities and challenges. In H. Hobohm (Ed.), *Knowledge* management: Libraries and librarians taking up the challenge (pp. 81–90). Munich, Germany: K. G. Saur.

Crow, R. (2002). SPARC institutional repository checklist and resource guide. Washington, DC: SPARC. www.sparc.arl.org/sites/default/files/IR _Guide_%26_Checklist_v1_0.pdf.

Downey, K., Zhang, Y., Urbano, C., & Klingler, T. (2014). Print book vs. DDA ebook acquisition and use at KSU Library. Technical Services Quarterly, 31(2), 139–160.

Farmer, L., & Safer, A. (2010). Developing California school library media program standards. School Library Media Research, 13. www.ala.org/ aasl/sites/ala.org.aasl/files/content/aaslpubsandjournals/slr/v0113/ SLR_DevelopingCalifornia_V13.pdf.

Fischer, K., et al. (2012). Give 'em what they want: A one-year study of unmediated patron-driven acquisition of ebooks. College and Research Libraries, 73(5), 469–492.

Galganski, C., & Thompson, J. (2008). Six Sigma: An overview and hospital library experience. Journal of Hospital Librarianship, 8(2), 133–144.

Garcia-Spitz, C. (2010). Applying MPLP to digitization: A project manager's perspective. Western Roundup Conference, Seattle, April 28–30.

Goben, A., & Raszewski, R. (2015). The data life cycle applied to our own data. Journal of the Medical Library Association, 103(1), 40–44.

Henczel, S. (2001). The information audit. Munich, Germany: K. G. Saur.

Hutt, A., Rose-Sandler, T., & Westbrook, B. (2007). Balancing the needs of producers and managers of digital assets through extensible metadata normalization. Against the Grain (Feb.), 41–43.

Jankowski, J. (2013). Successful implementation of Six Sigma to schedule student staffing for circulation service. Journal of Access Services, 10(4), 197–216.

Jantz, R. (2003). Information retrieval in domain-specific databases: an analysis to improve the user interface of the alcohol studies database. College & Research Libraries, 64(3), 229–39.

Kaplan, R., & Anderson, S. (2004). Time-driving activity-based costing. Harvard Business Review, 82(11), 131–138, 150.

Lockhart, J. (2014). Using item analysis to evaluate the validity and reliability of an existing online information literacy skills assessment instrument. South African Journal of Libraries and Information Science, 80(2), 36–45.

MacDonald, K. I., vanDuinkerken, W., & Stephens, J. (2008). It's all in the marketing: The impact of a virtual reference marketing campaign at Texas A&M University. Reference and User Services Quarterly, 47(4), 375–385.

McGurr, M. (2007). Improving the flow of materials in a cataloging department. *Library Resources and Technical Services, 52*(2), 54–60.

Murgai, S. (2006). Staffing needs of the reference desk at the University of Tennessee at Chattanooga: A statistical approach. *Public Services Quarterly, 2*(2–3), 167–190.

Nunnally, J. (1972). *Educational measurement and evaluation* (2nd ed.). New York, NY: McGraw-Hill.

Pande, P., Neuman, R., & Cavanagh, R. (2014). *The Six Sigma way: How to maximize the impact of your change and improvement efforts* (2nd ed.). New York, NY: McGraw-Hill.

Peters, T. (2015). Taking librarians off the desk: One library changes its reference desk staffing model. *Performance Measurement and Metrics, 16*(1), 18–27.

Pickett, C., Tabacaru, S., & Harrell, J. (2014). E-approval plans in research libraries. *College and Research Libraries* (March), 218–231.

Preiser, W. E., & Wang, X. (2006). Assessing library performance with GIS and building evaluation methods. *New Library World, 107*(5/6), 193–217.

Rossi, P. (2004). *Evaluation: A systematic approach.* Thousand Oaks, CA: Sage.

Roughneen, M. & Kinnear, J. (2015). Listen, talk, imagine: A case study of ethnography as a tool for school planning. *Independent School,* (Summer), 80–83.

Scharf, D. (2014). Instruction and assessment of information literacy among STEM majors. *Integrated STEM Education Conference, IEEE,* 1–7.

Soria, K. Fransen, J., & Nackerud, S. (2014). Stacks, serials, search engines, and students' success: first-year undergraduate students' library use, academic achievement, and retention. *Journal of Academic Librarianship, 40*(1), 84–91.

Stouthuysen, K., Swiggers, M., Reheul, A., & Roodhooft, F. (2010). Time-driven activity-based costing for a library acquisition process: A case study in a Belgian university. *Library Collections, Acquisitions, & Technical Services, 34,* 83–91.

Summer, D. (2007). *Six Sigma: Basic tools and techniques.* Upper Saddle River, NJ: Prentice-Hall.

Tidal, J. (2015). One site to rule them all: Usability testing of a responsively designed library website. *Association of College and Research Libraries conference proceedings,* Portland, March 26–28.

Turner, A. (2015). Implementation of batch cataloging: A case study. Association of College and Research Libraries conference, Portland, Oregon, March 25–28.

Vo-Tran, H. (2011). Adding action to the information audit. *The Electronic Journal of Information Systems Evaluation [Internet], 14*(2), 167–282.

Voyles, J. F., Dols, L., & Knight, E. (2009). Interlibrary loan meets Six Sigma: The University of Arizona Library's success applying process improvement. *Journal of Interlibrary Loan, Document Delivery and Electronic Reserves, 19*(1), 75–94.

Wheeler, D., & Chambers, D. (2010). *Understanding statistical process control* (3rd ed.). Knoxville, TN: SPC Press.

Wood, M. (2010). *The marketing plan handbook* (4th ed.). Englewood Cliffs, NJ: Prentice Hall.

Xia, J. (2005). Visualizing occupancy of library study space with GIS maps. *New Library World, 106*(5/6), 219–233.

Other Useful Reading

Glossaries of Statistical Terms:

- www.statista.com/statistics-glossary/A/
- www.stat.berkeley.edu/~stark/SticiGui/Text/gloss.htm

Bramer, M. (2013). *Principles of data mining* (2nd ed.). New York, NY: Springer.

Farmer, L., & Cook, D. (Eds.). (2011). *Using qualitative methods in action research: How librarians can get to the why of data.* Chicago, IL: American Library Association.

Foreman, J. (2013) *Data smart: Using data science to transform information into insight.* New York, NY: Wiley.

George, M., Rowlands, Dr., Price, M., & Maxey, J. (2005). *Lean Six Sigma pocket toolbook.* New York, NY: McGraw-Hill.

Hair, J. Jr., Black, W., Babin, B., & Anderson, R. (2009). *Multivariate data analysis* (7th ed.). Upper Saddle River, NJ: Prentice Hall.

Hernon, P., Dugan, R., & Matthews, J. (2015). *Managing with data: Using ACRLMetrics and PLAmetrics.* Chicago, IL: American Library Association.

Kenett, R., Zacks, S., & Amberti, D. (2014). *Modern industrial statistics: With applications in R, MINITAB and JMP* (2nd ed.). New York, NY: Wiley.

Larsen, R., & Marx, M. (2011). *Introduction to mathematical statistics and its applications* (5th ed.). Boston, MA: Pearson.

Maheshwari, A. (2014). *Data analytics made accessible.* Amazon Digital Services, Inc.

Mann, P. (2012). *Introductory statistics* (8th ed.). New York, NY: Wiley.

McDavid, J., & Hue, I. (2012). *Program evaluation and performance measurement* (2nd ed.). Thousand Oaks, CA: SAGE.

Mendenhall, W., & Sincich, T. (2011). *A second course in statistics: Regression analysis* (7th ed.). Boston, MA: Pearson.

Montgomery, D. (2012). *Introduction to statistical quality control* (7th ed.). New York, NY: Wiley.

Moore, D., McCabe, G., & Craig, B. (2014). *Introduction to the practice of statistics* (8th ed.). New York, NY: W. H. Freeman.

Pyzdek, T. (2003). *The Six Sigma handbook: The complete guide for greenbelts, blackbelts, and managers at all levels* (2nd ed.). New York, NY: McGraw-Hill.

Showers, B. (2015). *Library analytics and metrics: Using data to drive decisions and services*. London: Facet.

Stuart, D. (2014). *Web metrics for library and information professionals*. London: Facet.

Tague, M. (2004). *The quality toolbox* (2nd ed.). Milwaukee, WI: ASQ Quality Press.

Tan, P.-N., Steinbach, M., & Kumar, V. (2005). *Introduction to data mining*. Boston, MA: Pearson.

Xia, J. (2005). Visualizing occupancy of library study space with GIS maps. *New Library World, 106*(5/6), 219–233.

Wholey, J., & Hatry, H. (2010). *Handbook of practice program evaluation* (3rd ed.). San Francisco, CA: Jossey-Bass.

About the Authors

DR. LESLEY S. J. FARMER, professor at California State University, Long Beach (CSULB), coordinates the Librarianship Program. She earned her MS in library science at the University of North Carolina at Chapel Hill, and received her doctorate in adult education from Temple University. She has worked as a librarian in K–12 school settings, as well as in public, special, and academic libraries. She chairs the International Federation of Library Associations and Institutions' School Libraries Section and is a Fulbright Scholar. Dr. Farmer received the American Library Association Beta Phi Mu Award for distinguished service and library education, as well as several other professional association awards, and national and international grants. Farmer's research interests include information literacy, assessment, and educational technology, especially digital citizenship. A frequent presenter and writer for the profession, Farmer has published over 30 professional books and more than a 100 professional book chapters and articles.

DR. ALAN M. SAFER is a professor at California State University, Long Beach (CSULB), in the Department of Mathematics and Statistics. He received his PhD in Statistics from the University of Wyoming and his MS in Marketing Research from Southern Illinois University Edwardsville. He first came to CSULB as an assistant professor in 2000 and has been a full professor since 2010. Early in his career at the university, he created an MS degree in Applied Statistics and later a professional accelerated MS degree in Applied Statistics for industry students from companies such as Boeing, Raytheon, and Northrop Grumman. He served as the graduate advisor for 7 years, and in 2009 was awarded university advisor of the year at CSULB. Dr. Safer's research has been very interdisciplinary; he has over 25 publications in diverse statistical areas such as finance, library science, marketing, health science, linguistics, and forensics. His primary statistical research focus is data mining and quality control. In 2012, he was appointed coordinator of a national conference on quality control sponsored by the American Statistical Association. In the last few years, Dr. Safer helped create the Orange County/Long Beach chapter of the American Statistical Association and served as its vice president.

Contact the authors and join in the sharing of data and library analytics by visiting the authors' website: www.librarydataanalytics.com.

Index